P9-CJU-838

Trading Against the Crowd

John Wiley & Sons

Founded in 1807, John Wiley & Sons is the oldest independent publishing company in the United States. With offices in North America, Europe, Australia, and Asia, Wiley is globally committed to developing and marketing print and electronic products and services for our customers' professional and personal knowledge and understanding.

The Wiley Trading series features books by traders who have survived the market's ever-changing temperament and have prospered—some by reinventing systems, others by getting back to basics. Whether a novice trader, professional, or somewhere in-between, these books will provide the advice and strategies needed to help you prosper today and well into the future.

For a list of available titles, please visit our Web site at www.WileyFinance.com.

Trading Against the Crowd

Profiting from Fear and Greed in Stock, Futures, and Options Markets

JOHN SUMMA

John Wiley & Sons, Inc.

Published by John Wiley & Sons, Inc., Hoboken, New Jersey.
Published simultaneously in Canada.

For general information on our other products and services, or technical support, please contact our Customer Care Department within the United States at 800-762-2974, outside the United States at 317-572-3993 or fax 317-572-4002.

Wiley also publishes its books in a variety of electronic formats. Some content that appears in print may not be available in electronic books.

For more information about Wiley products, visit our web site at www.wiley.com.

ISBN: 0-471-47121-6

Printed in the United States of America.

10 9 8 7 6 5 4 3 2 1

For Lisa

The *efficient markets theory* asserts that all financial prices accurately reflect all public information at all times. In other words, financial assets are always priced correctly, given what is publicly known, at all times. Price may *appear* to be too high or too low at times, but, according to the efficient markets theory, this appearance must be an illusion.

—Robert J. Shiller
From *Irrational Exuberance*

Acknowledgments

This book could not have been written without the influence of earlier books that explored the role psychology plays in market price behavior long before I took up the quest. These include John Maynard Keynes's *The General Theory*, Charles Mackay's *Extraordinary Popular Delusions and the Madness of Crowds*, Humphrey B. Neill's *The Art of Contrary Thinking*, Norman Fosback's *Market Logic*, and Robert J. Shiller's *Irrational Exuberance*, to name only a few. I am indebted to these authors and their pioneering work.

I want to thank Pamela van Giessen of John Wiley & Sons for giving me the opportunity to make my own contribution to this tradition, as well as Lara Murphy and Jennifer MacDonald at Wiley for their professional handling of all my editorial concerns.

Also, I would like to express my gratitude for the superb copyediting done by Matthew Kushinka of PV&M Publishing Solutions, and the skillful translation of MetaStock code into TradeStation code by Ron Hudson.

While there were many other persons who helped me with this project, I would like especially to thank Lorie Meg Karlin of Managed Capital Advisory Group, Ltd. for her generous support during the final writing stages. I am also grateful to Bertrand Desruelles, Paltamas Gordon, Lisa Hardy, and John Sarich for their encouragement and valuable input at various stages of this project.

Contents

Preface

In his 1954 investment book classic *The Art of Contrary Thinking*, Humphrey B. Neill explained that the task of the contrarian "consists in training [the] mind to ruminate in directions opposite to general public opinions." In practice, this involves trading against prevailing market sentiment of what is popularly known as the investor "crowd."

Ruminating opposite the sentiment of the investor crowd, however, is not a subjective exercise. Today, this approach to the markets involves the use of objective market indicators that attempt to gauge investor and trader sentiment as accurately as possible, most importantly to identify when they reach extremes. *At extreme levels of market sentiment the market tends to be most predictable, the best precondition for taking a trade.*

After years of watching, researching, and trading the markets, I still find measures of investor sentiment to be my most reliable and thus favorite indicators. I am not alone in my experiences. Many successful traders and money managers place special emphasis on investor sentiment gauges to inform their trading decisions. And so should you.

In this book, I explain how to understand investor sentiment data, build custom indicators with that data, and incorporate these sentiment indicators in trading systems that I have developed and tested.

While the premise of this book is that the speculative crowd tends to misread the market at the *most* extreme sentiment points, some of the trading systems presented here also profit from less extreme sentiment. Profitable trading is shown to be possible in above- and below-average bearish and bullish sentiment cycles that operate within larger sentiment waves. Whether trading on short-term cycles (or waves) or longer-term ones, however, the systems tested and presented here provide powerful evidence of the nonrandom (thus, predictable) nature of markets.

While markets ultimately may be regulated by fundamentals, the common errors and misjudgments that regularly appear in the crowd's actions suggest another dimension to market price behavior is at work. It appears markets become victim of the crowd's emotions for periods of time longer than random walk theorists (who believe that predicting future price movements is not possible) are willing to accept. Examples of these crowd actions are the manias found in history like the stock market bubble of the 1990s, as well as short-term overreaction to news shocks. The goal of this book, therefore, is to develop trading systems that are capable of harnessing profitably such emotionally charged misjudgments.

Finally, it is my hope that this book inspires you to begin your own ruminations against the crowd. The trading systems and custom sentiment indicators presented in this book do not represent the final word on this subject. Hopefully, these will encourage you to explore similar approaches—perhaps discovering even better ways to extract profit by trading against the sentiment of the investor crowd.

JOHN SUMMA
New Haven, CT

April 2004

Introduction

I first discovered the power of investor sentiment indicators when I began tracking daily put and call option volume during the bull market of the 1990s. One of the most followed and reliable sentiment gauges, and one given special emphasis in this book, is the Chicago Board Options Exchange (CBOE) equity-only put/call ratio. It began sending warning signals of an impending market decline in late 1999 and early 2000, a development I conveyed to readers of my OptionsNerd.com weekly market report at that time.

The extreme readings showed excessive bullishness that was reflected in low CBOE put/call ratios (demand for call options had significantly increased relative to put options). This came on top of a palpable breakdown of technical conditions in equity markets, adding weight to the argument that it was time to get out. Too many call options demanded relative to puts indicates a complacent market, vulnerable to potential disturbances. The crowd, a term that is used in this book to refer to emotionally driven investors with less sophistication, became too uniform in their view of the market, believing stocks could only keep rising.

Investors or traders who expect a rise in prices purchase call options. Put options are purchased in anticipation of a fall in prices. The lack of interest in put options, therefore, along with the surging demand for call options (reflected in a low put/call ratio), showed a lack of concern about the potential for downside stock market price movement. I need not recount the end of this story, as events that followed in 2000, 2001, and 2002 speak loudly enough to the power and immense value of this timely indication.

Used correctly, therefore, sentiment indicators can produce excellent market timing signals capable of pinpointing short- and medium-term market tops and bottoms. In this book, I incorporate put/call ratios, as well as other gauges of crowd psychology—option volatility, short sales, investor surveys, advisory opinion, and news flow—into trading systems that I have developed, such as Squeeze Play I and II and Tsunami Sentiment Wave, (for which I have presented MetaStock and TradeStation system code in Appendices A and B). The results establish beyond any doubt, that sentiment, if properly harnessed, remains an excellent trading tool.

That said, the potential to deliver profits depends on the discipline that traders bring to the game, along with the use of effective money management to handle signals that are false. Trading systems fail mostly because traders fail to follow the rules, but they can also suffer from periodic drawdowns when the signal accuracy misfires. So even a good trader can suffer from periodic failure of even the best indicators and systems. The ability to manage drawdowns largely separates the successful trader from the rest of the pack. When you plan your trades, therefore, be sure to tenaciously trade your plan if you want to survive.

CONTRARY OPINION VERSUS CONTRARY INVESTING

Many books have been written about contrary opinion in regards to investing. Actually, many of the original works in the area of investor sentiment are from a long-term *investing* perspective, and largely examine the issue through contrarian analysis of stock market fundamentals, such as P/E (price-to-earnings) ratios. This book ignores fundamentals and instead focuses only on what I call *sentiment technicals:* put/call ratios, option volatility, short sales, advisory opinion, investor surveys, and quantitative news flow (my own contribution to the field, which is covered in Chapter 19). By using these sentiment measures, it is possible to identify investor sentiment extremes and associated market turning points.

A unique dimension to this book is the combination of price triggers with sentiment gauges. Sentiment is rarely enough information for a trading system but does provide an excellent initial screen for trading. On their own, sentiment indicators too often tend to give premature signals. As I demonstrate in this book, however, performance improves dramatically by applying simple price-based triggers for timely entering of a trade at times of extreme investor sentiment. This secondary set of conditions for a trade significantly increases the hit rate of the trading systems I present in this book. The use of technical price triggers is thus an important contribution for sentiment technicians to consider, a term I use to refer to technical analysts who place great weight on measures of crowd psychology or investor sentiment in their trading approaches.

IS CONTRARY TRADING FOR YOU?

The biggest obstacle associated with using sentiment data and the systems presented in this book is the difficulty of taking trades when the majority, including most professionals, is betting the other way. With a consensus of opinion bullish, for example, you have a system telling you everybody else is wrong, and that you should get into a bearish position. This is clearly not for the faint of heart. You are going completely against the prevailing thinking, often against the so-called experts, which is akin to charging headlong into the running bulls in Pamplona, Spain.

This approach, therefore, requires a solid belief in your trading plan, and the ability to stand alone against the crowd. While this approach might not be for everybody, it does offer potential profits for those with the fortitude and determination to take positions in anticipation of a trend change. This occurs when the investor crowd shifts its opinion, and the market reversal now becomes your tailwind as buyers turn into sellers en masse at market tops, or sellers almost miraculously disappear or turn into buyers at market bottoms.

The frequency and reliability of this pattern—and how to capitalize on it—is the subject of this book.

CHAPTER 1

Reflections of a Contrarian on Investor Psychology

Being a market contrarian might seem contrary to common sense. Why fight *against* the prevailing mood of the market and its associated momentum? Recall the old trader adage "the trend is your friend," which certainly has merit. But what happens if the trend is about to come to an end? Then the trend becomes a trap, unless you are carefully tracking market sentiment, which can help you spot an upcoming trend change.

Market sentiment is the most important force in market moves, not fundamentals, and the logic is not too difficult to grasp. The age-old truism that "a thing is worth only what someone else will pay for it" today can be found operating in the "greater fool" theory of price behavior: Stock prices keep rising only because somebody else remains willing to buy at a higher price. As a contrarian and sentiment technician, watching the crowd become "greater fools" is my business. For example, I attempt to profit from overly bullish crowd moods as the prevailing bullish trend suddenly shifts, and the stock market crumbles like "castles in the air," to quote the famous economist John Maynard Keynes. Keynes was describing the more important emotional or psychological factors—as opposed to intrinsic or fundamental values—that drive markets ever higher during times of investor optimism. During pessimistic bouts the same dynamic is at work.

I have found that by properly tracking and assessing investor psychology, it is possible for the astute trader or investor to make above-average profits and, in some instances, exceptional profits.

Sentiment technicians try to take the temperature of both the average investor and the trading crowd in hopes of finding an advantageous entry point just before an old trend ends and a new one begins. Therefore, by *trading against the crowd* at times of extremely bullish or bearish market sentiment, contrarians aim to get in early on the start of a *new* trend, which follows a market reversal. Should their prediction be realized, contrarians are positioned to gain from the development and continuation of this new trend until it becomes ripe for reversal, following another manic swing of investor sentiment to the opposite side of the bull–bear spectrum.

Contrarian sentiment technicians, therefore, do not have a problem with trends per se. Instead, they simply attempt to spot the zone where the prevailing trend is likely to end. Spotting these zones of excessive bullish (overbought) or bearish (oversold) investor sentiment is a crucial precondition in my trading systems presented in this book. This trading approach can produce spectacular profits, as I demonstrate through rigorous back testing on numerous stock and futures markets. This testing incorporates my custom sentiment indicators, which are explained in subsequent chapters.

The kind of inefficiency shown to exist through investor sentiment analysis and trading systems tests in this book should rankle diehard believers in efficient markets. Systematic, wrongheaded investor or trader sentiment is difficult to refute as a powerful trading technique. This occurs because it captures periods when the market has become dominated by emotions, as opposed to the textbook mechanism of perfect price adjustments for all known information.

THE THEORY OF CONTRARY OPINION

The theory of contrary opinion has a revered status among traders and investors. As already mentioned, the approach involves measuring crowd psychology and trading against the crowd at sentiment extremes. This offers one essential advantage over other technical approaches. Unlike most technical analysis, sentiment technicians incorporate *non-price data* streams (such as put/call volume ratios alluded to earlier) into their models to aid in market timing.

Predicting market tops—and bottoms—is never easy, but enough successful sentiment technicians and traders exist to prove that the theory of contrary opinion has long-lasting merit. The most notable fact is that these market inefficiencies and profitable trading patterns, evident from an analysis of market psychology, while well known to smart traders and investors, are not easily arbitraged away, as adherents to efficient markets theory would have us believe. These inefficiencies and patterns may persist and can never disappear for very long due to the nature of the crowd.

The basic theory is simple: If, during bullish markets, nearly all market participants hold and act upon bullish opinions, then prices are likely to decline. The premise is that everybody who can be in the market already is, and if the view underpinning the crowd's behavior turns out to be wrong, then everybody is wrong—just when things seem so right. This can produce a quick reversal of the trend, as buyers suddenly turn into sellers. The same dynamic applies during periods of panic selling. Markets reverse when sellers have been exhausted, often in combination with a sudden revision of the economic story and an end to the prevailing pessimism. The selling is said to have gotten "overdone" and the market turns higher, often fueled by short sellers who scramble to "cover" (buy back) their short positions. Some attribute this identifiable pattern in the history of stock and futures prices to the amateurish behavior of the crowd.

However, today with markets dominated by mutual fund managers, who are considered the professionals, it is difficult to make the case that the theory of contrary opinion depends solely on the nonprofessional. When market participants act as a group either excessively bearish or bullish, their level of experience and capital is irrelevant. Therefore, while many technicians (including this one) emphasize the crowd as the less sophisticated trader or investor against whom the "smart" money trades, I believe that today the crowd may at times be defined in broader terms; we can include some of the professional traders and investors who are tempted to go with the momentum for a number of compelling reasons. Recall the behavior of fund managers and stock market analysts during the bull market bubble of the late 1990s; these so-called professionals repeatedly forecast the market incorrectly while investing other people's money on their predictions.

FINDING INEFFICIENT MARKETS

Looking back at market booms and busts of the past century, one discerns a behavioral pattern that can be measured in psychological terms. While the late 1990s stock market bubble is the most recent example, it by no means represents the only case where long-term deviations from an imputed fundamental or intrinsic value occurred. This need not be considered only in terms of mega-bubbles. Historic speculative bubbles and episodes of run-for-the-exits panic selling are evident in short-to-medium-term cycles as well, which this book seeks to identify and profitably exploit.

Crowd psychology can exhibit short-, medium- and long-term excesses, as there are many traders and investors with different time horizons built into their market approaches. Short- or long-term trend changes can be associated with certain degrees of public delusion, short-term excessive bullishness or bearishness, some degree of detachment from economic and financial fundamentals, or equilibrium prices, often fostered by small and large waves of fear or greed. Investors, for example, might pile into a stock following a positive news surprise; this leads to a very short-term overly bullish position in the issue, against which some short-term traders may attempt to trade.

The theory of contrary opinion has applications, therefore, in many time frames. In fact, an entire body of economic theory called behavioral finance has emerged to explain the fact that prices appear to move about largely in response to common misjudgments about the market rather than to accurate, instantaneous adjustments to new information. This results in continuous over- or undershooting of what might be thought of as equilibrium fair value. This can happen for a very short or a very long period, and for great distances.

The efficient markets hypothesis, whose important corollary for traders states that it is impossible to systematically predict price behavior using trading systems that incorporate historical data (because markets are said to follow a random walk), maintains that prices are always efficient, reflecting the fundamental (discounted net present) value of an asset. Prices that conform to a "random walk" pattern (that is, have no foreseeable path) cannot be predicted using technical patterns or trading systems. According to random walk theorists, traders who rely on already known information, or "stale" news, which has already been discounted, are doomed to fail.

The premise of my approach is that patterns of short-, medium-, and long-term common misjudgments or errors made by the investment community exist. Recall that random walk market theory implies that it is not possible to consistently beat the market by using any past information, and that all the time, money and energy devoted to this business is pure folly. But if markets are not efficient *all* the time due to limited arbitrage, or lack of arbitrage, and people periodically take leave of their senses as they get caught up with the crowd (including possibly the pros) for whatever reason, then random walk arguments fail to explain such excessively bullish or bearish market movements.

Investor sentiment gauges, indicators, and trading systems presented in this book, including my new quantitative news flow indicator, thus appear to offer a serious challenge to the school of efficient markets and random walk theory. Human nature appears to limit the ability of investors to act on investment psychology measures even when they are aware of them. After all, the theory of crowds is such that individuals are more influenced by others than objective measures of what others are doing.

WHAT MARKETS WORK BEST WITH CONTRARIAN APPROACHES?

Because analysis of investor psychology attempts to locate bullish and bearish sentiment extremes (where markets historically have reversed direction and changed their prevailing trend), any market that has heavy participation by the retail public would be the most likely place to apply the strategies I present in this book. The hypothesis is that the greater the degree of participation by the nonprofessional public, the more likely it is that the crowd will follow a herd instinct. Due to reduced transaction costs associated with ownership of personal computers and improved Internet access over the past eight years, the amateurish crowd is arguably more involved than ever before in trading and investing (particularly in the options markets). This makes contrarian trading strategies more powerful than ever.

Analysis of investor or trader psychology can take many forms. A common denominator of this approach to trading is the use of an objective method to assess market moods and a market's vulnerability to a trend change, which in this book is viewed in short- to medium-term time frames. Typically, market sentiment measures are looked at historically for high and low extremes that correspond to market turning points. Given past levels of these gauges, it is possible to incorporate these wave-like patterns into trading systems.

As I have already explained, the theory of contrary opinion is based on the historical fact that markets tend to over- and undershoot equilibrium levels and are thus not *always* efficient . This is due to an investing or trading crowd prone to a herd mentality, largely driven by emotion rather than fundamentals. It is when this subjective factor (emotion) gets too far out of line with objective factors (technicals and fundamentals) that markets become ripe for reversals. The crowd is very often wrong just when all seems right—a recurrent pattern this book will explore systematically.

Once a sentiment extreme is identified, timely entries into the market can be made in hopes that these are near market tops or bottoms. Therefore, levels of extreme elation (buying) or panic (selling) become signals for getting positioned to catch the end of a trend. As a result, there is a certain resistance to applying the theory that may not be suitable for those who need to follow the prevailing view.

SUMMARY

Human nature is such that most people need to be emotionally secure in their decisions, which is precisely why they get pulled along with the herd, even if they are aware of objective analysis telling them to do otherwise. They choose to ignore history and thus capitulate to the herd mentality. And capitulation is key. Without it, there would be no emotional extremes in the short or long term, and thus no trading possibility for a system based on these sentiment extremes.

Market participants are assumed by efficient markets devotees to know better than to push prices too far. Yet this is why sentiment indicators have held up so well while many other indicators have become valueless. People cannot help but be human, with all its failings, especially when it comes to matters of making (or losing) money. Human fallibility is one constant that guarantees that this approach will always remain an effective one, although indicators may need to be updated or changed to provide the best measure for what the crowd is thinking and doing. Group behavior is a powerful psychological factor that reinforces why trading against the crowd will remain a viable approach to beating the markets.

CHAPTER 2

Measuring "Joe Options Trader" Sentiment

Options traders are not known for their market acumen. Despite the perennial flow of books published on how to trade options successfully, success appears as elusive as ever for this crowd. Options traders today, despite ever more powerful software and data feeds, cheaper and faster trading platforms, and educational tools, remain inadequate at the trading game. They are so bad, in fact, that the options crowd has been, and is likely to remain, a valuable source of data for sentiment technicians.

Invented by Marty Zweig in 1971, the put/call volume ratio indicator is still used by traders to determine when the options trading crowd is on a call-buying or put-buying binge. When too much buying has been identified, with the options crowd tilted too far one way in their sentiment (buying too many puts or calls), you can usually bank on a nearby market reversal. This is hardly the stuff of random walk theorists who believe the markets and their participants efficiently price markets.

The data is now available for most individual stocks and in the aggregate from a number of vendors. The huge expansion in exchange-listed options volume during the past 20 years, particularly with the online options trading boom brought on largely by the growth of the Internet, provides an excellent, accessible source of investor and trader sentiment. These traders make highly leveraged, poorly timed bets on what they think will be short- to medium-term market directions on which the options trade. Bullish options traders purchase call options to bet on an anticipated market rise; bearish options traders buy put options to speculate on a perceived decline in markets. Call options rise in value if the underlying stock

Stk	Opt	Name	Call	Put	Total Volume	Days	Total ADV	Call ADV	Put ADV
CSCO	CYQ	Cisco Systems, Inc.	301,610	124,302	425,912	20	21,296	15,081	6,215
C	C	Citigroup, Inc.	117,989	237,783	355,772	20	17,789	5,899	11,889
GNTA	GJU	Genta Incorporated	142,471	144,798	287,269	20	14,363	7,124	7,240
MSFT	MQF	Microsoft Corporation	187,473	76,649	264,122	20	13,206	9,374	3,832
INTC	INQ	Intel Corporation	156,153	86,702	242,855	20	12,143	7,808	4,335
NT	NT	Nortel Networks Corporation	162,586	60,475	223,061	20	11,153	8,129	3,024
GE	GE	General Electric Company	152,764	63,878	216,642	20	10,832	7,638	3,194
AMR	AMR	AMR Corporation	120,731	79,622	200,353	20	10,018	6,037	3,981
TASR	QUR	TASER International, Inc.	89,574	85,095	174,669	20	8,733	4,479	4,255
HPQ	HWP	Hewlett-Packard Company	99,484	75,120	174,604	20	8,730	4,974	3,756
MO	MO	Altria Group, Inc.	64,089	96,625	160,714	20	8,036	3,204	4,831
EBAY	QXB	eBay, Inc.	60,274	84,656	144,930	20	7,247	3,014	4,233
AMAT	ANQ	Applied Materials, Inc.	79,269	65,597	144,866	20	7,243	3,963	3,280
NYB	NQK	New York Community Bancorp	92,926	45,900	138,826	20	6,941	4,646	2,295
JPM	JPM	J.P. Morgan Chase & Co.	88,559	47,528	136,087	20	6,804	4,428	2,376
DAL	DAL	Delta Air Lines, Inc.	70,589	63,220	133,809	20	6,690	3,529	3,161
TWX	AOL	Time Warner, Inc.	98,450	33,044	131,494	20	6,575	4,923	1,652
YHOO	YHQ	Yahoo! Inc.	59,970	71,148	131,118	20	6,556	2,999	3,557
DELL	DLQ	Dell Computer Corp.	66,605	64,396	131,001	20	6,550	3,330	3,220
IBM	IBM	International Business Machines Corporation	75,150	52,192	127,342	20	6,367	3,758	2,610
TXN	TXN	Texas Instruments Incorporated	72,695	53,885	126,580	20	6,329	3,635	2,694
NXTL	FQC	NEXTEL Communications, Inc. (Class A)	85,056	36,123	121,179	20	6,059	4,253	1,806
EP	EPG	El Paso Corporation	57,254	54,510	111,764	20	5,588	2,863	2,726
CPN	CPN	Calpine Corporation	49,293	59,750	109,043	20	5,452	2,465	2,988
BRCM	RCQ	Broadcom, Inc.	68,734	37,383	106,117	20	5,306	3,437	1,869
WMT	WMT	Wal-Mart Stores, Inc.	62,633	43,137	105,770	20	5,289	3,132	2,157
HD	HD	Home Depot, Inc. (The)	58,068	37,605	95,673	20	4,784	2,903	1,880
ELN	ELN	Elan Corporation PLC ADR	70,740	23,252	93,992	20	4,700	3,537	1,163
GS	GS	The Goldman Sachs Group, Inc.	70,183	22,880	93,063	20	4,653	3,509	1,144
GM	GM	General Motors Corporation	38,934	49,611	88,545	20	4,427	1,947	2,481
LU	LU	Lucent Technologies, Inc.	65,530	22,899	88,429	20	4,421	3,277	1,145
NOK	NOK	Nokia Corporation ADR	55,710	31,924	87,634	20	4,382	2,786	1,596

FIGURE 2.1 CBOE Top 100 Equity Options—May 2003. (*Source:* CBOE.)

increases in value. Put options, meanwhile, gain value if the underlying stock price declines. Since only a fraction of the value of the stock or stock index is required to buy options, these financial instruments act as surrogates for owning the actual stock (or stock index). Figure 2.1 presents a snapshot of the top 100 CBOE equity options markets, including each stock's average daily call and put volume (ADV).

Options markets attract the least capitalized and typically least experienced traders. If IBM is trading at $45 per share, for example, and you expect it to rally higher, you could buy a short-term at-the-money call option (the equivalent of 100 shares of IBM) to speculate on the anticipated move. Let's say the option costs $5.00 in premium. This would cost you $500 because equity options have standardized terms whereby $1.00 in premium is the equivalent of $100, so a $5.00 call option costs you $500.

Instead of buying the stock itself for $4,500 ($45 × 100 shares), you can speculate on the move higher for just $500. If IBM moves to $50 fast enough, the option will have increased to approximately $750, a 50 percent profit, assuming a Delta value of .5 (the Delta value is the percentage an option price moves given a percentage change in the underlying). Had you bought the actual stock instead, your profit would be just 2.5 percent! The catch is that options are wasting assets (they decay over time), and the premium declines with each passing day. Therefore, the bets are always made within certain expected lengths of time as determined by expiration dates of the option contract.

WHAT DOES OPTIONS TRADING VOLUME TELL US?

The presumption here is that options market sentiment is a good indicator for the overall investment mood of the market.When options volume increases it suggests more speculative fervor. If this volume is concentrated in puts then the fervor is bearish; if it is in calls then the trader mood is bullish. Most equity options are traded by inexperienced speculators who make bets primarily on the direction of stocks and certain stock indices, like the Dow Jones, NASDAQ and S&P 500. More recently, the introduction of exchange traded funds (ETFs) and options on ETFs has fostered another area of highly liquid equity index speculation.

The options on the triple QQQs (NASDAQ 100 ETF) are typically seen among the most active list on any given trading day. Figure 2.2 presents a snapshot of the most active equity options and index contracts at the Chicago Board Options Exchange (CBOE), one of the leading equity options exchanges. The September 38 QQQ call option was the leader on this particular day with 58,582 contracts traded. Figure 2.3 illustrates how active the QQQ puts can be. The top six contracts traded on this day were July and September QQQ puts.

By creating a ratio of daily put volume divided by daily call volume, we in effect have a bear/bull sentiment intensity ratio. The put/call ratio will fall to extreme lows when there is a preponderance of call buying. When there is strong bearish sentiment, reflected in increased demand for puts relative to calls, the put/call ratio rises to extreme highs. Remember, the theory of

CLASS	VOLUME	HIGH SERIES	VOLUME	LAST SALE	CHANGE
QQQ	388,705	C SEP 38	58,582	1.00	- .10
S P T	61,894	P JUL 1100	5,578	5.00	+ .60
OEX D	52,878	C JUL 560	9,883	2.45	- .75
TASR	46,293	C JUL 45	5,019	3.50	+ 1.20
IWM A	36,409	P AUG 111	26,147	1.75	- 1.75
SPQ AM	18,644	P DEC 1050	2,708	24.60	+ 1.20
YHOO	18,613	P JUL 35	5,241	1.10	- .50
DIA	15,738	C JUL 105	1,873	.60	- .20
ELAN	14,652	C JUL 25	3,205	.70	+ .15
DJX O	14,577	C SEP 104	3,252	3.00	+ .15
MSFT	13,752	C JUL 27 1/2	4,041	1.00	- .20
INQ	10,766	C OCT 27 1/2	3,316	1.60	- .25
DELTA	10,588	C AUG 7 1/2	5,233	.70	+ .20
MQG 06	9,849	C JAN 10	9,839	.65	+ .10
TTN	9,827	C AUG 12 1/2	4,120	1.60	+ .20
CSCO	9,046	C AUG 22 1/2	2,062	1.65	
DAL 06	8,766	P JAN 5	5,606	2.25	- .15
MO	8,074	C JUL 55	1,983	.05	- .05
QXB B	7,919	P JUL 90	1,043	1.45	- .45
S X B	7,915	P SEP 950	3,566	3.40	+ .20
ABS 06	7,625	P JAN 25	7,625	2.70	- 2.20
NFLX	6,707	P SEP 35	1,234	4.50	- 2.80
ELX	6,613	C AUG 15	4,315	.70	- .30
AAQ	6,377	P JAN 30	2,785	2.15	+ .30
SZP AM	5,951	C SEP 1200	2,775	7.00	- .30
GEN EL	5,419	P JUL 32 1/2	880	.50	+ .15
UPS	5,217	C OCT 80	2,544	.35	+ .10
WALMAR	4,811	P JUL 55	1,505	2.65	+ .45
RUL A	4,792	C AUG 85	775	.55	+ .10
SNDK	4,602	P OCT 20	1,501	1.85	+ .45
MO 05	4,590	C JAN 55	3,414	1.35	+ .45
ASKJ	4,496	P SEP 40	1,540	5.30	- 1.00
EBAY	4,469	P JAN 30	3,000	.05	
HD	4,456	P JUL 35	3,814	.40	+ .05
TEX IN	4,338	C JUL 25	3,032	.30	- .05
KMRT	4,315	P AUG 55	1,648	.65	- .10
NT 06	4,185	C JAN 12 1/2	2,300	.25	- .05
AMR	4,179	C JAN 15	2,674	1.25	+ .20
IMCL	4,052	C JUL 85	533	2.30	+ .30
JPM 05	4,030	P JAN 37 1/2	2,000	2.60	+ .05
NOK	3,997	C OCT 15	1,114	.75	+ .05
MOT 07	3,900	P JAN 10	3,900	.65	- .20
AMZN	3,846	C JUL 45	993	8.90	+ 2.20
C	3,834	P SEP 45	1,027	1.15	+ .25
XMSR	3,640	C JUL 27 1/2	919	.25	+ .05

FIGURE 2.2 CBOE most active list—July 13, 2004. (*Source:* CBOE.)

contrary opinion says that when traders become too bullish (low put/call ratio) or too bearish (high put/call ratio), they are often wrong and the market makes a reversal.

Figure 2.4 illustrates this relationship, whose data plots take the shape of a butterfly. The inverse relationship is easy to interpret. The lower plot shows the CBOE equity put/call ratio and the upper plot shows the S&P 500 stock index. At market peaks (S) the options put/call ratio shows valleys, and vice versa (L).

In Figure 2.4, a CBOE equity put/call ratio series has been smoothed with a 21-day exponential moving average. Other time frames can be used to meter the mood of traders and investors, which I explain further in subsequent chapters when presenting my custom indicators. To effectively monitor the mood of the options crowd, the raw data series typically needs to be smoothed using moving averages to reduce unnecessary market "noise." The best raw data time frame I have found is the *daily* put/call ratio, but I examine which of the three popular categories of put/call ratios in this time frame works best in Chapter 4. I examine the CBOE equity-only, CBOE total, and OEX index options put/call ratio series (options that trade on the S&P 100).

	SERIES	VOLUME	LAST SALE	CHANGE
QQQ	SEP 38	58,582	1.00	- .10
QQQ	JUL 38	52,275	.25	- .05
QQQ	JUL 36	45,041	1.35	- .20
QQQ	SEP 36	42,586	2.40	+ .05
QQQ	JUL 37	41,467	.60	- .20
QQQ	SEP 37	36,569	1.75	+ .15
OEX D	JUL 560	9,883	2.45	- .75
MQG 06	JAN 10	9,839	.65	+ .10
OEX D	JUL 555	8,598	4.30	- .70
OEX D	SEP 580	5,955	3.90	- .60
DELTA	AUG 7 1/2	5,233	.70	+ .20
TASR	JUL 45	5,019	3.50	+ 1.20
ELX	AUG 15	4,315	.70	- .30
TTN	AUG 12 1/2	4,120	1.60	+ .20
MSFT	JUL 27 1/2	4,041	1.00	- .20
TASR	JUL 50	3,900	2.00	- .35
YHOO	JUL 35	3,823	1.70	+ .45
OEX D	JUL 565	3,740	1.30	- .40
S P T	SEP 1140	3,478	28.10	- 2.90
MO 05	JAN 55	3,414	1.35	+ .45
QQQ	JUL 37	47,132	.60	+ .10
QQQ	DEC 37	33,103	1.95	- .30
IWM A	AUG 111	26,147	1.75	- 1.75
QQQ	JUL 38	8,601	1.15	+ .10
ABS 06	JAN 25	7,625	2.70	- 2.20
QQQ	SEP 35	6,170	.75	+ .10
DAL 06	JAN 5	5,606	2.25	- .15
S P T	JUL 1100	5,578	5.00	+ .60
YHOO	JUL 35	5,241	1.10	- .50
S P T	SEP 1140	4,211	31.00	- 1.00
MOT 07	JAN 10	3,900	.65	- .20
HD	JUL 35	3,814	.40	+ .05
S P T	JUL 1125	3,643	10.90	+ .70
S X B	SEP 950	3,566	3.40	+ .20
TASR	JUL 40	3,315	2.95	+ .20
S P T	JUL 1120	3,276	9.40	+ .90
QQQA06	JAN 35	3,275	3.00	+ .05
OEX D	JUL 550	3,275	6.90	+ .90
S P T	SEP 1100	3,171	19.00	- 1.20
PFE 06	JAN 35	3,000	3.70	+ .40

FIGURE 2.3 CBOE most active all-put series—July 13, 2004 (*Source:* CBOE.)

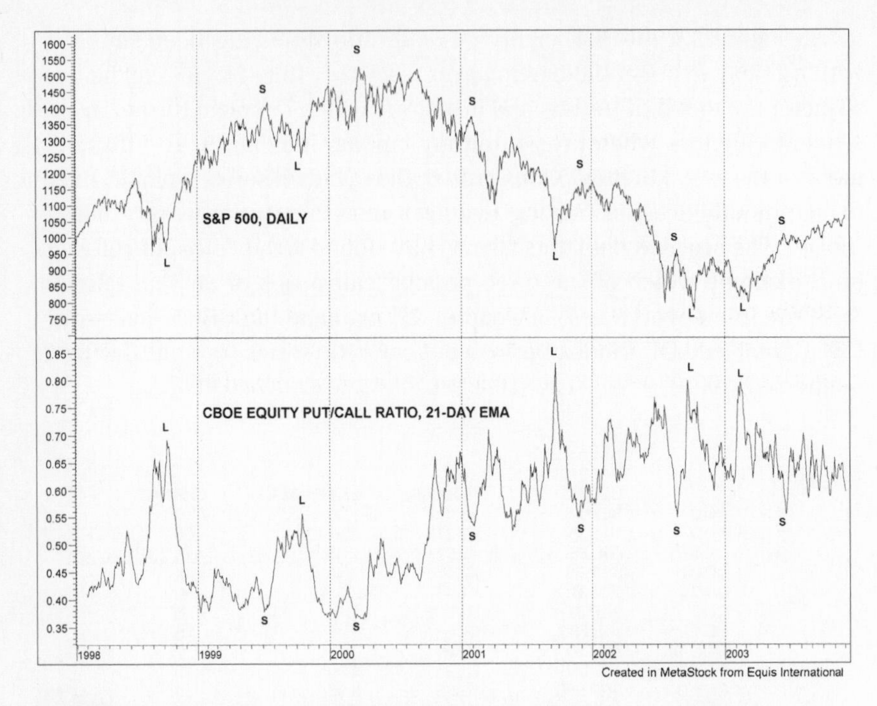

FIGURE 2.4 CBOE equity put/call ratio chart with 21-day exponential moving average. L's represent buy points and S's sell points. (*Source:* Pinnacle Data.)

It is not entirely clear why these indicators work so well. The most widely held belief is that options markets, especially the buy side of that market, attract the least experienced traders, who tend to have less capital. Given these two factors, I believe they are most likely to make bad trading decisions. Of course, many professional traders can also be wrong about the market. Regardless of trader experience or capitalization levels, if the options trading crowd is increasingly of consensus opinion about the market direction and is making the same directional bets, before long the market will prove it wrong. History has shown this statement to be correct.

It may not always be the so-called unsophisticated trader that gets it wrong, as mentioned previously. When there is too much put buying relative to call buying (or vice versa), the market will experience a reversal—no matter who is doing the trading. In fact, it might be that when the professional crowd is also drawn into the herd mentality, the best signals arise. The majority opinion, therefore, is usually wrong at the sentiment extremes, no matter who joins the group.

As such, it would appear that speculative trading sentiment does not discriminate. It is not that the crowd is less sophisticated, it is simply the fact that when extremes are reached in levels of put buying during bearish periods (and call buying during bullish periods), the market has reached a point of extreme vulnerability. The reversal comes about because there are no sellers left in the case of bear declines, and no buyers left during bull rallies. In these circumstances, there is little to prevent the market from rapidly reversing since with few or no sellers in a bear decline (and many potential buyers and short coverers), there is a great opportunity for buyers (for example, short covering). Similarly, having no buyers in a bull market can be a great opportunity for sellers (bulls get squeezed out).

SUMMARY

While there is no definite answer as to exactly why, the fact remains that put/call ratios have proven to be very reliable indicators. The implication this has for efficient markets theory—a theme I allude to from time to time throughout this book—is rather serious. Since the theory says that it is not possible to profit from trading systems and historical data of any kind, using historical data such as put/call ratios would thus be pointless, for they should offer no forecasting value. But if the past behavior of the options crowd has identifiable patterns of emotional extremes associated with market reversals, and this can be programmed into a trading system to produce above-average profit rates, what does this say about so-called efficient markets? Clearly, astute traders who resist the influence of the options crowd, and go against that crowd at the right time, have an edge in the trading game. The next three chapters examine this claim, with some surprising discoveries about the exact nature of the options crowd.

CHAPTER 3

Will the Real Put/Call Ratio Please Stand Up?

Since Marty Zweig first introduced and popularized the put/call ratio concept, there have been attempts to refine and improve the original method, with mixed results. This chapter provides a brief description of the different forms of the put/call ratios used by sentiment technicians for assessing the mood of the options crowd.

The Chicago Board Options Exchange weekly put/call ratio, a measure of all of the options activity at the CBOE, was used exclusively through 1985 and still continues to be the most widely quoted. Even though most traders consider the daily number much more effective, *Barron's* Market Laboratory section continues to publish just the weekly numbers. A reading below 40 was once indicative of too little interest in calls, thus the market was a buy. Conversely, a reading above 65 was thought to signify too little interest in puts, so the market was a sell. Today, fixed levels of the indicator are no longer useful due to trendiness in the data over the long term, and most traders resort to a more dynamic data reading, looking at the most recent extremes and how they correspond with market turning points. Later in this book, I present a simple custom indicator that transforms a raw daily series into an oscillator that removes troublesome longer-term trends in the data.

With the growth of other exchanges—particularly the huge success of the all-electronic International Securities Exchange (ISE), which touts its tighter market (referring to spreads between bid and ask prices)—the value of the CBOE data as a proxy of total options trading may be somewhat diminished. I have not seen any deterioration, however, of the predictive power of the CBOE options.

Interestingly, though, the ISE daily options volume (topping one million each day) as seen in Figure 3.1 in theory may offer a better measure of the

RELATED LINKS

Exchange Volume by Symbol
Most Active Issues/Series
Products Traded

QUOTES

Stocks
Options

DATA TABLE -- [5/24/2004 to 6/28/2004]

Date	Trades	Volume	Calls	% Calls	Puts	% Puts
05/27/04	69,845	1,310,397	757,433	58%	552,964	42%
05/26/04	73,015	1,352,225	853,089	63%	499,136	37%
05/25/04	91,908	1,724,124	1,054,128	61%	669,996	39%
05/24/04	86,530	1,254,103	772,307	62%	481,796	38%
AVERAGE*	71,926	1,247,782	727,890	58%	519,892	42%
TOTAL*	1,726,215	29,946,762	17,469,356	58%	12,477,406	42%

FIGURE 3.1 ISE options trading statistics. (*Source:* From ISE website.)

options trading crowd than the CBOE due to its heavy use by the small retail customer using point-and-click pure electronic trading architecture. Recent phenomenal growth can be seen in ISE equity options volume, particularly the options on the QQQs, which are the most liquid as well as the most active daily options contracts. The ISE opened for trading in May 2000 and in three years overtook the other established exchanges, becoming the leader in equity options volume. (ISE began trading index options on October 3, 2003.)

This makes the ISE options volume the most likely place to find our unsophisticated options trader. However, at this point there is too short an historic data series for back testing and evaluation of ISE options traders in isolation. Perhaps in the future it will provide an even better source of sentiment data than the CBOE put/call ratio volume.

As mentioned earlier, the daily volume numbers offer the most valuable information about the options trading crowd. Figure 3.2 provides a snapshot of the CBOE's daily market statistics page located at their excellent website.

Figure 3.2 shows the CBOE total put/call ratio at .87 on June 29, 2004. This includes index options as well as equity options, so the total number is "polluted" by professional options trading volume, which is linked to portfolio manager hedging with put index options and use of short (covered) call options to offset the cost of purchasing puts. Many sentiment technicians prefer the equity-only put/call ratio, which is a derivative of the CBOE total ratio, to get a better read of the speculative crowd. Figure 3.2 shows the equity-only put/call ratio at .77 and the index put/call ratio at 1.42. Later in the book, I do some comparative tests on the performance of equity-only options put/call ratio data and a subgroup of index options traders using the OEX (S&P stock index) options put/call ratio to see if it is possible to

CBOE Market Summary for Tuesday, June 29, 2004

Total Put/Call Ratio				0.87
Index Put/Call Ratio				1.42
Equity Put/Call Ratio				0.77
				Close
BXM				649.45
	Open	**High**	**Low**	**Close**
VIX	15.22	16.28	15.22	15.47
	Open	**High**	**Low**	**Close**
VXO	16.45	16.45	15.37	15.37
	Open	**High**	**Low**	**Close**
VXN	20.46	20.52	19.90	20.15

Sum of All Products

	Call	Put	Total
Volume	589137	511491	1100628
Open Interest	70307511	59697513	130005024

FIGURE 3.2 Market statistics page at CBOE. (*Source:* CBOE.)

identify smarter versus less sophisticated groups of traders. In addition, I compare these to the total CBOE ratio.

Typically there are a smaller number of put options traded on any given day than there are call options, with the CBOE equity put/call daily ratio, as seen in Figure 3.3, swinging quite wildly. It reached above 1.0 on bearish days (lots of put buying) and sank below .5 on bullish days (lots of call buying). Above the daily series, I have placed a smoothed 10-day exponential moving average (10-DEMA) that shows two different periods of ranges—those corresponding to a bull market and those corresponding to a bear market. These ranges (low and high) moved higher during the bear market, as can be seen in Figure 3.3. Typically during a bull market, the ratio ranges from .35 (low) to above .45 (high). During the bear market (2001 foreword), the low-end ranges are closer to the previous high-end ranges. This structural break in the series points to the need to remove the long-term trend in this data to allow for the creation of more stable short-term threshold values for analysis, a point I return to later in this book.

Typically, the index option put/call volume ratio is higher than the equity-only put/call ratio, reflecting the heavy use of put options by portfolio managers. Figure 3.4 shows the historical pattern for this ratio, both daily and smoothed versions (10-DEMA). Note that the smoothed series rarely gets below 1.0 and sometimes reaches above 2.0, quite different ranges than seen for equity-only put/call ratios. Later I examine what these extremes mean in terms of market turning points. For now, I want to move on to issues pertaining to which ratio might work best for market timing and system trading.

As mentioned earlier, the CBOE total put/call ratio captures the combinations of both equity option put and call volume, as well as index option put and call volume. Many sentiment technicians, however, believe that the CBOE ratio is distorted by the growing use of index put options by portfolio managers to hedge large stock positions, since they hardly represent the moody crowd. Equity options growth on the QQQs, along with diminished use of the OEX index options by the same speculators, would appear to further this line of thinking. Options on ETFs, like the QQQs, have mushroomed, which are counted as equity options.

With the growth of ETFs and options on ETFs, the OEX has become less important for the retail options trading crowd looking to trade equity indices. This is especially true with better bid ask prices on the options on

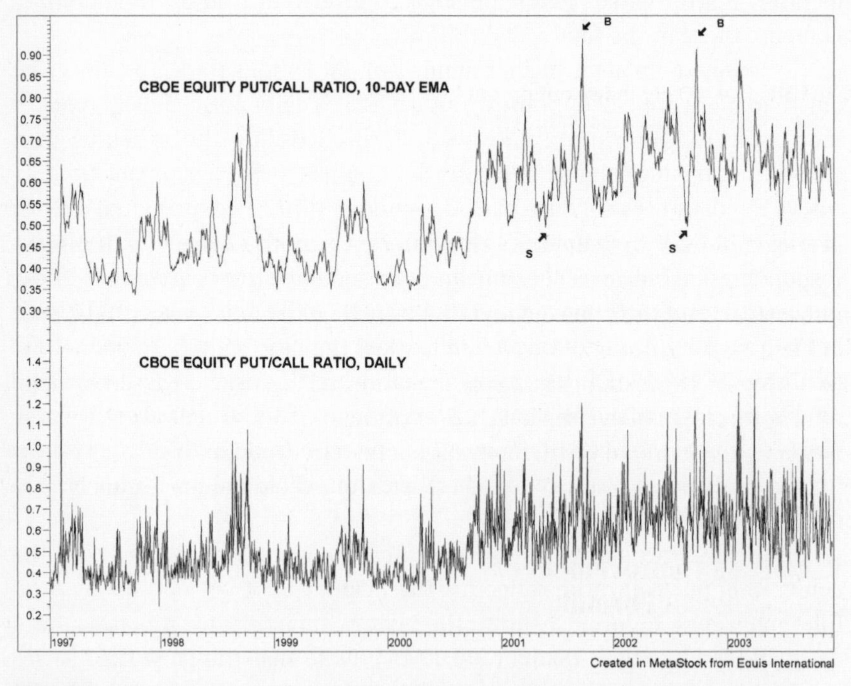

FIGURE 3.3 Daily equity-only put/call ratio and smoothed series.Spikes above 1.0 on the daily ratio represent bearish extremes. Below .5 typify bullish days.

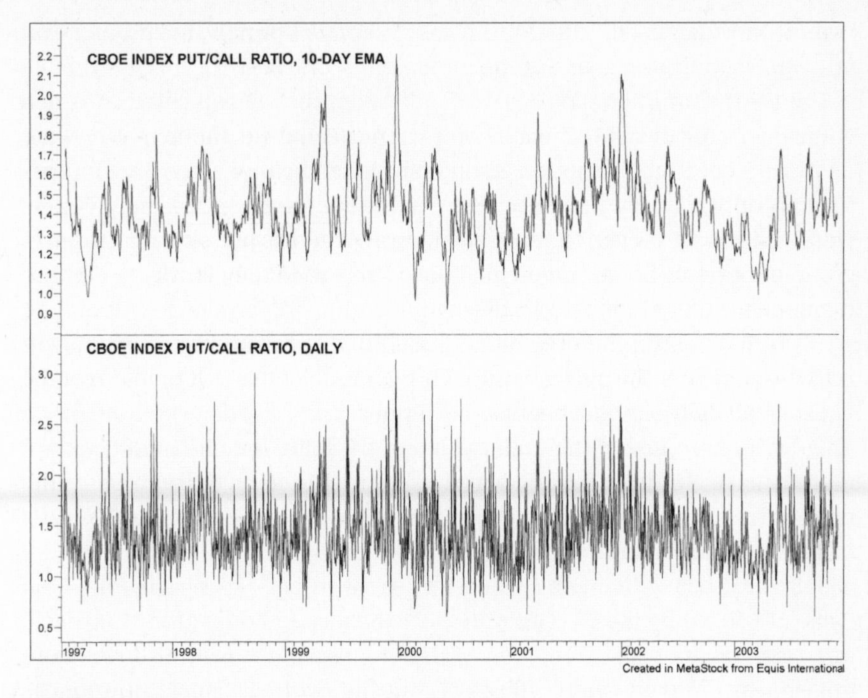

FIGURE 3.4 Daily index option put/call ratio and smoothed series. Daily spikes higher can sometimes top 3.0, extreme bearishness.

ETFs. Combined with index option hedging, mentioned earlier, it would appear that the best measure of the pure trader crowd is the equity-only option volume. Again, this includes the hugely popular options on the QQQs and less popular but still significant options on Diamonds (options on the Dow Jones ETF). With better bid/ask spreads these markets have exploded.

Therefore, I believe the best gauge of the mood of the unsophisticated options trading crowd is still the equity-only put/call ratio of the CBOE—or, better yet, the equity-only put/call ratios of all exchanges combined.

Attempted Improvements of the Standard Put/Call Ratio Formula

Having covered some basic issues surrounding the traditional CBOE put/call ratio, I want to review some of the methods that sentiment technicians have developed to improve the original concept regardless of what volume is being used. There are a few variations worth mentioning that attempt to improve the use of the indicator.

Since the traditional put/call ratio does not distinguish between which volume is being measured, each contract gets equal weight no matter what its price. Therefore, an option traded far out-of-the-money costing far less than an option trading near or at the money (or even in the money) gets weighted equally—even though much more money is at risk with the latter group of options. Some traders feel that this is not the best way to capture the mood of the options trading crowd.

A refinement to the original approach that is favored by some traders is to dollar-weight the put/call ratio. This approach creates a ratio not of the put and call daily *volume*, but instead of the put and call daily options *value*. The theory here is that the dollar value of the daily options traded gives a more accurate picture of the degree of bearishness or bullishness of the options trading crowd. For example, let's say we have 75 puts and 100 calls traded. The put/call ratio would be .75. But assume that the 100 calls were significantly out-of-the-money calls, let's say worth 50 cents each, for a total value of $50, while the 75 puts were near the money bought for $1.00 each, or a total value of $75. Here we see that the *volume* measure shows more bullishness (75 puts versus 100 calls) but the *value* measure shows more bearishness ($75 in puts versus $50 in calls). More money is bet on the bearish side using the dollar-weight approach than the volume-based put/call ratio, thus giving a false impression of the sentiment of the options trading crowd.

I have some problems with this approach. I have tested trading systems, which are presented later in this book. They do not provide a systematic improvement in performance using dollar-weighted averages, even though they may offer advantages to some traders depending on how they are applied. One issue with dollar weighting is that an in-the-money option that has a lot of dollar value is going to be given greater weight in the calculation, even though it may represent a portfolio hedger. Note that many unsophisticated traders tend to buy cheaper, out-of-the-money options because they get more leverage (and have less capital), which is what attracts them to options trading in the first place. Perhaps the best approach would be one that compares dollar-weighted out-of-the-money options. Otherwise, I am not convinced that dollar-weighted put/call ratios offer as great an edge as some might think.

Most sentiment technicians have rejected the use of static put/call ratio threshold levels. Noted options trading expert Larry McMillan argues, for example, that static levels used as buy or sell points should be avoided in favor of a dynamic approach, such as looking for local maxima or minima on the charts. A simple way to look at threshold levels is to use a 52-week high-and-low of a moving average of the series. Another method is to look at the recent history of the smoothed series to determine the best levels to use. There are many other ways to do this that are beyond the scope of this book. I prefer a simple detrending method, obtaining the difference of a faster and slower moving average to provide a more stable range to examine.

McMillan's shift to a dynamic approach followed the failure of the traditional CBOE total put/call ratio to predict the October 1987 stock market crash. He attributes this to massive put buying by portfolio hedgers in the months ahead of Black Monday, which actually pushed total put/call ratio levels to buy points right ahead of the crash. For this reason, he prefers the use of dynamic levels, as well as a put/call ratio purged of index options volume, leaving an equity-only put/call ratio series.

An additional method aimed at improvement is the Hines Ratio, named after its creator, Ray Hines. It compares related volume data to open interest levels. This weighting scheme uses open interest levels for calls and puts. This approach essentially looks at the daily call volume in relation to open interest for calls, and the daily volume for puts in relation to open interest in puts. By incorporating open interest into the traditional put/call volume ratio, the Hines Ratio attempts to capture relative intensity of put or call volume in terms of open interest.

Sentiment technicians also developed another ratio that uses put/call *open interest* to indicate the response of the options trading crowd. More open interest in puts might suggest greater bearishness and vice versa. I have not found open interest data to be easy to interpret, however, and find that there are conflicting views about exactly what the open interest represents.

Still another technique involves selecting just near the money strikes for inclusion in the construction of the daily put/call ratio data series. Some technicians prefer to use options that are within a certain percentage range of the money (the price of the underlying), or to use only the volume of the at-the-money options which can be dollar-weighted or a simple contract volume ratio to gauge the speculative crowd's mood. The hypothesis is that the short-term traders prefer to buy near-the-money options because that is where they will get the biggest gains should their prediction about market direction be correct. Options that are just out of the money have a high gamma value, meaning that delta will sharply increase with a quick market move in the desired direction, especially if they are right at the money, thus raising the price of the option rapidly. These calculations, however, are difficult to do. I prefer to stick with the traditional data, using volume only.

Finally, increasingly traders watch intraday put/call ratios. Figure 3.5 contains these CBOE equity and index option put/call volume ratios, which are updated every 30 minutes during market hours. Intraday ratios are not the focus of this book; my experience, however, has been that when the intraday ratio of total CBOE options goes above 1.0 for several 30-minute sessions, especially near key support levels for the major averages, strong rallies often ensue. I have seen this repeatedly and encourage you to test this idea, as it might hold tremendous value for day traders.

So far we have discussed the use of put/call ratios for the broad market averages. The same indicators, however, can be similarly applied to individual stocks and certain futures markets. If the markets are sufficiently liquid for options, which is the case for most large-cap stocks, the option put/call ratio might work to predict market tops and bottoms in your favorite technology stock or Dow component, for example. Not all futures and stocks, however, have the same success rate. If you attempt to apply these indicators to markets, you should try to diversify as much as possible

Half Hourly Exchange Volume Report For 6/29/2004

		Equity			Index			Total		Put / Call
Time	Calls	Puts	Total	Calls	Puts	Total	Calls	Puts	Total	Ratio
9:00 AM	41334	33123	74457	8411	17790	26201	49830	50913	100743	1.02
9:30 AM	81386	77936	159322	16320	34958	51278	97824	112897	210721	1.15
10:00 AM	135107	122316	257423	23470	42031	65501	158708	164350	323058	1.04
10:30 AM	167342	143466	310808	29431	48143	77574	196922	191613	388535	0.97
11:00 AM	192773	158250	351023	38682	58115	96797	231615	216369	447984	0.93
11:30 AM	219052	175116	394168	45879	69528	115407	265108	244648	509756	0.92
12:00 PM	260932	213185	474117	51738	72589	124327	312862	285778	598640	0.91
12:30 PM	299817	254527	554344	54397	74653	129050	354425	329184	683609	0.93
1:00 PM	324357	273476	597833	59759	81709	141468	384388	355195	739583	0.92
1:30 PM	364627	301104	665731	62890	90496	153386	427832	391610	819442	0.92
2:00 PM	394205	322640	716845	67141	98940	166081	461691	421590	883281	0.91
2:30 PM	428880	346842	775722	70817	103217	174034	500042	450069	950111	0.9
3:00 PM	494071	380330	874401	84407	113369	197776	578823	493709	1072532	0.85

FIGURE 3.5 CBOE intraday put/call ratios. Bullish signal given with three 30 minute readings above 1.00. (*Source:* CBOE.)

to improve overall performance, as some markets can outperform others and some not do well at all. That said, I limit my testing of custom indicators and trading systems in this book to a small group of randomly selected big-cap stocks, stock indices, and in futures markets to the long bond.

SUMMARY

In the previous chapter I introduced the basic theory of put/call ratios as one method used to measure investor sentiment and to trade against the crowd. In this chapter, I surveyed the standard put/call ratio approaches and some alternative formulations that have been developed to improve measurements of trader sentiment. The daily equity-only put/call ratio, in my opinion, remains the best series to use in trading against the crowd, despite numerous attempts to find better measures of the options trading crowd. In Chapter 4, I compare the ability of the equity-only put/call ratio with the CBOE total and OEX put/call ratios to predict the equity market's medium-term tops and bottoms.

CHAPTER 4

The Options Trading Crowd at Extremes

Equity-only put/call ratios have the most intuitive appeal for sentiment technicians looking to keep a finger on the pulse of the nonprofessional crowd, the most likely traders to make common misjudgments among options traders as a group. If the equity-only options traders are in fact wrong when the group thinks alike at sentiment extremes, it should be easy to examine this options trading crowd behavior to see if it has any reliability and special patterns that would be useful for trading system development.

In this chapter, therefore, I conduct a series of tests of the conventional equity-only put/call ratio option volume data to determine if the options trading crowd is predictably wrong in its trading decisions near sentiment extremes. The tests show the degree to which this data series provides reliable information about the short- and medium-term direction of the S&P 500 following excessive bearish or bullish sentiment captured in put/call ratio levels.

While I do not develop any trading system as such in this chapter, the work here lays the foundation for developing trading systems later in the book. For now, I turn to an examination of the power of this data series to predict future stock market direction.

CONSTRUCTION OF THE CONVENTIONAL EQUITY-ONLY PUT/CALL INDICATOR

Generally, put/call ratios are constructed from daily data using a "smoothing method" to wring out excessive market noise. Most traders prefer an exponential moving average instead of a simple moving average because it can be configured to put more weight on the more recent data used in the moving average calculation. A simple moving average applies the same weight to each of the values in the calculation, which is considered to be less reliable. Typically, 10- and 21-period exponential moving averages are used for daily data, and 4- and 8-period exponential moving averages used on weekly data. The tests I employ use a 10-period exponential moving average, for consistency and comparative purposes, when working with daily data in this and the next several chapters.

To take this smoothing idea one step further, I difference a short- and long-term exponential average of the raw daily series to create an oscillator that shows percentage deviation from the longer-term average (EMA 10-250). I subtract the 10-day period from the 250-day period exponential moving average to accomplish the detrending of the daily put/call ratio series, and convert it to a percentage deviation from the 250-day average. This is easy to do in a spreadsheet program or software like MetaStock Professional. These percentage deviations can then be examined for emotional extremes, which on their own, often provide excellent signals for trading against the crowd.

EXAMINATION OF CBOE DAILY EQUITY PUT/CALL RATIO SPIKES

This chapter will look at the CBOE equity-only put/call ratio in its EMA 10-250 oscillator form. This ratio moves in a butterfly pattern that is opposite to the direction of the stock market. In other words, when the stock market is bullish, investors are purchasing more calls relative to puts, and the ratio falls. When the market is bearish, investors and traders buy more puts relative to calls; this will push the put/call ratio higher. This is evident in Figure 4.1, where well-defined spikes higher can be seen near market bottoms. Figure 4.2, meanwhile, shows well-defined spikes lower corresponding to market tops. The spikes represent percentage deviations from the average level of sentiment registered over the previous 250 days.

Later I use key findings and insights from these simple tests and develop them into a trading system. The trading systems use this important secondary data stream run in custom indicators in combination with simple, price-based triggers.

To evaluate the equity-only put/call volume ratio in its EMA 10-250 oscillator form, I examine these key threshold levels for both buy and sell

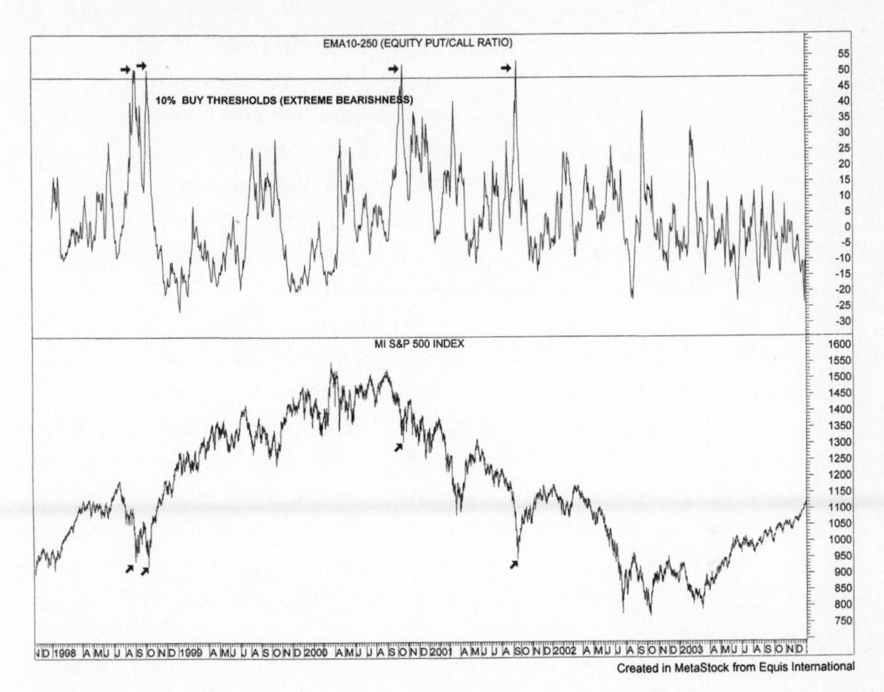

FIGURE 4.1 Extreme bearish buy thresholds using equity-only put/call EMA 10-250. (*Source:* Pinnade Data.)

signals. These levels are consistently applied to all the indicators in the sample tests on put/call ratios to provide a comparative basis for assessing the predicative power of these investor sentiment measures. Remember, at this stage, I am only interested in determining the relative predictive power of put/call ratios that will be studied: equity-only, CBOE total, and OEX. Recall that the premise of this book is that at emotional extremes, the majority is usually wrong. If markets have become overly bullish or bearish at these extremes, traders can capitalize on a reversal that should follow these emotional excesses.

It would be interesting, although difficult, to quantify the amount of money lost by options traders at these turning points. Clearly, however, casual observation provides enough evidence to suggest that many options buyers are throwing their money to the wind, as seen in Figures 4.1 and 4.2. In a study of options expiration by the Chicago Mercantile Exchange, furthermore, during a three-year period (1997–1999), over 95 percent of all S&P 500 put options on futures expired worthless, and it was even worse

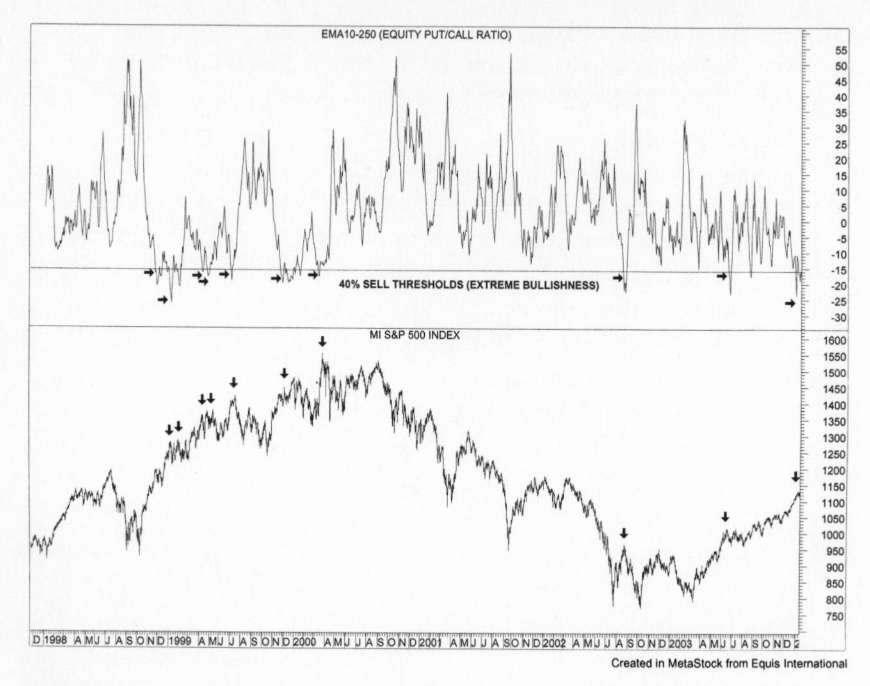

FIGURE 4.2 Extreme bullish sell thresholds using equity-only put/call ratio EMA 10-250 oscillator. (*Source:* Pinnacle Data.)

for the NASDAQ 100 options. Meanwhile, call options traders did better, but clearly still lost on average.

EXTREME BEARISHNESS THRESHOLD LEVEL ANALYSIS

The S&P 500 cash index will be used for evaluating the three-put/call ratios series just mentioned.

I use six key percentage thresholds: 10, 15, 20, 30, 40, and 50. These are not percentile ranks. Instead, I simply analyze price changes in different time frames beginning on days that register extreme put/call ratio threshold levels. For example, the 10 percent threshold level evaluates all days when the oscillator value is within 10 percent of its highest high (following which I expect to see bullishness) and 10 percent of its lowest low (following which I expect to see bearishness). Using this information, price changes in percentage terms are then measured over a range of future time intervals to determine both the probability of the expected direction occurring and by what percentage.

Let's say the equity-only put/call ratio's EMA 10-250 oscillator's maximum value in the study period is 53.41 and the lowest value is –26.46. We would calculate the 10 percent buy threshold level by taking values above 48.01. To derive this threshold, I multiply the maximum level (53.41) by .10 and then subtract this amount (5.341) from the maximum level, leaving 48.01 (the 10 percent buy threshold value). Positive values are buy levels and negative values sell thresholds.

The sample period for equity put/call ratios runs from January 6, 1998 (the raw data actually extends further back) to January 28, 2004, but since we need to create a 250-day moving average to detrend the data, we lose a year of data in the sample for testing. In addition, since we are forward-testing the threshold levels over different time frames, we do not have use of the data to the latest date in the series. The loss of data depends on the testing time frame. The same limitations apply to the CBOE total put/call ratio as well. That said, the number of days in the testing period is 1,283 for equity-only put/call ratios.

The results of a 10 percent buy threshold level, which produced excellent results in nearly all time frames, are presented in Table 4.1. It contains the time frames T + 5 (5 days after threshold penetration) through T + 240 (240 days after penetration of a threshold). Overall, the extreme sentiment threshold levels produced an average change in price of 5.31 percent in the T + 40 and shorter time frames. The average change in price rose to 12.03 percent in the T + 50 and longer time frames. Comparing these results with the historical random average change in the price of the S&P 500 during these same time frames, seen in Table 4.1, there is no question that it pays to trade against the options trading crowd when these traders become excessively bearish. The average change in price of the S&P 500, for example, is just .33 percent for the shorter time frames and .45 percent during the longer time frames, a significant difference.

In terms of probability, a move in the intended direction for the extreme sentiment buy threshold level (that is, too much bearishness) shows strong results as well. Table 4.2 contains data showing that for the T + 40 and shorter time frame averages, in terms of probability of a price move, the average for the entire group is 77.55 percent compared to an his-

TABLE 4.1 Percentage Change in Price of S&P 500 Following Penetration of Extreme Bearish Sentiment Thresholds

Sentiment Thresholds	T + 5	T + 10	T + 20	T + 30	T + 40	% Totals
10	5.3	7.39	6.9	7.48	12.16	7.85
15	3.97	6.46	6.37	6.84	10.74	6.88
20	3.41	5.59	5.44	5.1	8.7	5.65
30	2.43	4.08	5.19	6.47	9.37	5.51
40	0.8	2.39	3.22	4.36	6.87	3.53
50	0.27	1.24	2.25	3.36	5	2.42
Threshold Average	2.7	4.53	4.9	5.6	8.81	**5.31**
Historical Average	0.1	0.19	0.35	0.46	0.54	**0.33**
Sentiment Thresholds	**T + 50**	**T + 60**	**T + 120**	**T + 180**	**T + 240**	**% Totals**
10	14.43	18.3	22.04	24.71	21.55	20.21
15	11.87	15.45	16.93	18.95	13.55	15.35
20	8.69	11.57	10.18	13.01	6.4	9.97
30	10.14	12.43	12.37	15.43	9.98	12.07
40	8	8.93	9.68	11.41	7.29	9.06
50	5.75	5.68	6.1	6.68	3.5	5.54
Threshold Average	9.81	12.06	12.88	15.03	10.38	**12.03**
Historical Average	0.57	0.61	0.6	0.55	–0.08	**0.45**

Source: Summa Capital Management and Research. Thresholds are derived from CBOE equity-only put/call ratio EMA 10-250 oscillator values.

torical random average probability of a price rise during this period of 53.3 percent. Results presented in Table 4.2 for longer time frames further confirm the predictive power of the equity put/call ratio, with an overall threshold penetration probability of a price rise of 65.76 percent versus a 48.68 percent random probability of a price rise during the same period.

Clearly, therefore, when the crowd is in a panic (indicated by high threshold levels of the EMA 10-250 oscillator), it is the time to buy the stock market, not sell, as most investors are mistakenly doing (or buying puts if an options trader).

A closer look at the data reveals some valuable information. If we take individual thresholds and time frames, a pattern of decreasing probability is

TABLE 4.2 Probability of S&P 500 Stock Index Price Rise Following Penetration of Extreme Bearish Sentiment Thresholds

Sentiment Thresholds	T + 5	T + 10	T + 20	T + 30	T + 40	% Totals
10	100	100	100	85.7	85.7	94.28
15	83.3	100	83.3	83.3	83.3	86.64
20	80	100	80	66.7	80	81.34
30	71	90.3	74.2	71	77.4	76.78
40	56.4	70.9	67.3	63.6	70.9	65.82
50	52.3	60.2	60.2	63.6	65.9	60.44
Threshold Average	73.83	86.9	77.5	72.32	77.2	**77.55**
Historical Average	52.8	52.3	54.2	53.4	53	**53.14**

Sentiment Thresholds	T + 50	T + 60	T + 120	T + 180	T + 240	% Totals
10	85.7	85.7	85.7	85.7	71.4	82.84
15	75	75	75	75	58.3	71.66
20	60	60	60	60	46.7	57.34
30	74.2	71	64.5	67.7	58.1	67.1
40	72.7	65.5	58.2	61.8	52.7	62.18
50	65.9	58	47.7	50	45.5	53.42
Threshold Average	72.25	69.2	65.18	66.7	55.45	**65.76**
Historical Average	52.8	52.7	47.9	47.5	42.5	**48.68**

Source: Summa Capital Management and Research. Thresholds are derived from CBOE equity-only put/call ratio EMA 10-250 oscillator values.

apparent as we move from less extreme levels of the equity put/call ratio. This makes sense as the options trading crowd is less uniform and has mixed emotions at less extreme levels. The best overall performance in terms of percentage price change is in the T + 180 time frame, with an average rise in price of 15.03 percent (with an associated 66.7 percent probability of a price rise). The highest probability of a price rise time frame is T + 10, with an 86.9 percent probability of a price rise (with an associated average rise in price of 4.53 percent). The historical random average for this threshold and time frame is 52.3 percent and .19 percent, respectively—significantly less.

As for perfect probability scores, there were a total of 5, one at the 20 percent threshold level, one at 15 percent, and three at 10 percent. The T + 10 time frame produced three 100 percent threshold levels (10, 15, and 20), where all days following penetration of buy threshold levels produced rising prices.

EXTREME BULLISHNESS THRESHOLD LEVEL RESULTS

Moving to the sell-side threshold, a somewhat different pattern of performance is evident. Overall, the power of the equity put/call ratio is substantially reduced. Both the probability of success and percentage price change measures significantly underperform the buy-side thresholds that were just reviewed. While part of this is no doubt due to the historical bullish bias of stocks, it may also have to do with other unknown factors.

As seen in Table 4.3, on average all shorter-term time frames (≤ T + 40) show modest results in the desired direction (bearish prices), but the performance deteriorates as time elapses. While there is one winning threshold at T + 50 days, the remainder in the T + 50 and greater time frames show prices rising, not falling. This no doubt reflects the fact that market declines typically are short-lived, although during the study period, the number of bearish years (2000, 2001, 2002) is equal to the number of bullish years (1998, 1999, 2003), so one would have expected better results here since the sample is balanced between bull and bear years.

On an overall basis, the T + 40 and shorter time frames yielded an average of –1.23 percent per trade. But for the T+50 and longer time frames, the performance is not good. Here, we have an average rise in price of 3.51 percent. The best threshold was the 15 percent level for selling, when the S&P 500 during ≤ T + 40 declined in percentage terms from a low of –1.69 percent to a high of –4.50 percent, or an average of –2.31 percent. As for probabilities, the overall probabilities of a price fall for the ≤ T + 40 time frames did beat the historical average for any given day during the study at 61 percent versus 46.9 percent. But during the ≥ T + 50 time frames seen in Table 4.3, the chance of a price fall following penetration of sell threshold levels (extreme bullishness), was just 23.5 percent, less than half the random probability percentage probability of price fall (51.2 percent).

Taking a look at the longer time frames, there is a deterioration of performance. The only profitable time frame was T + 50, a decline of the

TABLE 4.3 Probability of S&P 500 Price Fall Following Penetration of Extreme Bearish Sentiment Thresholds

Sentiment Thresholds	T + 5	T + 10	T + 20	T + 30	T + 40	% Totals
10	100	100	100	100	0	80
15	71.4	66.7	100	80	40	71.62
20	69.2	77.8	100	46.2	33.3	65.3
30	50	54.4	54.8	60	50	53.84
40	50.5	50	45.5	57.5	47.1	50.12
50	49.1	47.7	46.7	52.7	44.2	48.08
Threshold Average	65.03	66.1	74.5	66.07	35.77	**61.49**
Historical Average	37.3	37.6	35.4	36.3	36.9	**36.7**

Sentiment Thresholds	T + 50	T + 60	T + 120	T + 180	T + 240	% Totals
10	50	0	0	0	0	10
15	40	20	20	25	0	21
20	33.3	22.2	22.2	25	0	20.54
30	43.3	43.3	20	22.2	22.2	30.2
40	39	31	24.7	18.8	30	28.7
50	35.8	30.9	26.6	23.3	35.6	30.44
Threshold Average	40.23	24.57	18.92	19.05	14.63	**23.48**
Historical Average	37.1	37.1	42.9	43.4	49.4	**41.98**

Source: Summa Capital Management and Research. Thresholds are derived from CBOE equity-only put/call ratio EMA 10-250 oscillator values.

S&P 500 on average of –.45 percent, and less than 50 percent success rate (only two of the seven cases were successful). The average change of the S&P for the entire T + 50 time frame and longer came in at 3.05 percent, not a very good showing, since we are looking here for price declines. However, this 15 percent threshold clearly did not produce an average rise in the S&P 500 that warrants taking a long position. Compared to the 15 percent buy threshold level, the low levels of bearishness measured in the low readings on the equity-only EMA10-250 oscillator should at least keep you out of a long position until more favorable conditions arise.

SUMMARY

Using options trading crowd behavior in the form of CBOE equity-only put/call ratios, penetration of extreme bearishness thresholds led to price changes of the S&P 500 that easily beat random price changes and probabilities. On penetration of sell threshold levels, however, results were mixed, with the shorter time frames studied beating the random probability and percentage price changes. The longer time frames (greater than T + 50 days) that followed an extreme sell threshold penetration showed inferior performance.

CHAPTER 5

Does the Entire Group of Options Traders Get it Wrong?

If the equity-only put/call volume ratio is considered representative of "Joe Options Trader" sentiment, then the index options trader crowd, many who are professional money managers, might be described as "smart" money. Whether index options traders are less likely to be wrong at market extremes than the nonprofessional traders, however, is not entirely clear. In this chapter, the CBOE total put/call ratio is subjected to the same testing conducted in the previous chapter. Since the total ratio includes all options traders, the presence of professional index options traders might cause the ratio to be less predictive of future price changes.

EXTREME THRESHOLD LEVEL ANALYSIS

Figures 5.1 and 5.2 illustrate the bullish and bearish threshold levels of the CBOE total put/call ratio EMA10-250 oscillator. They exhibit the same spikes of extreme sentiment seen in the previous chapter and correspond to market turning points. Clearly, the pattern is similar enough to suggest that the options crowd as a whole gets it as wrong as the equity-only options traders. Subjecting this EMA10-250 oscillator to the threshold tests confirms this pattern. At all major market bottoms there are significant spikes higher, almost identical to what was seen in the previous chapter.

Following penetration of buy threshold levels by the CBOE total put/call ratio EMA10-250 oscillator, there was an overall average rise in the price of 5.91 percent, compared with a random rise in the price of just .32 percent

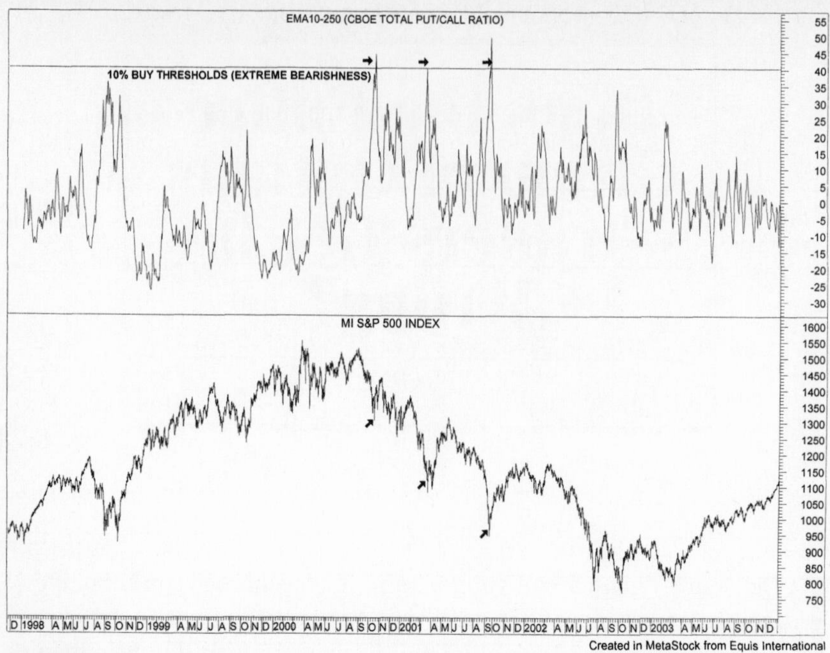

FIGURE 5.1 Extreme bearish sentiment thresholds using CBOE total put/call ratio EMA10-250 oscillator. (*Source:* Pinnacle Data.)

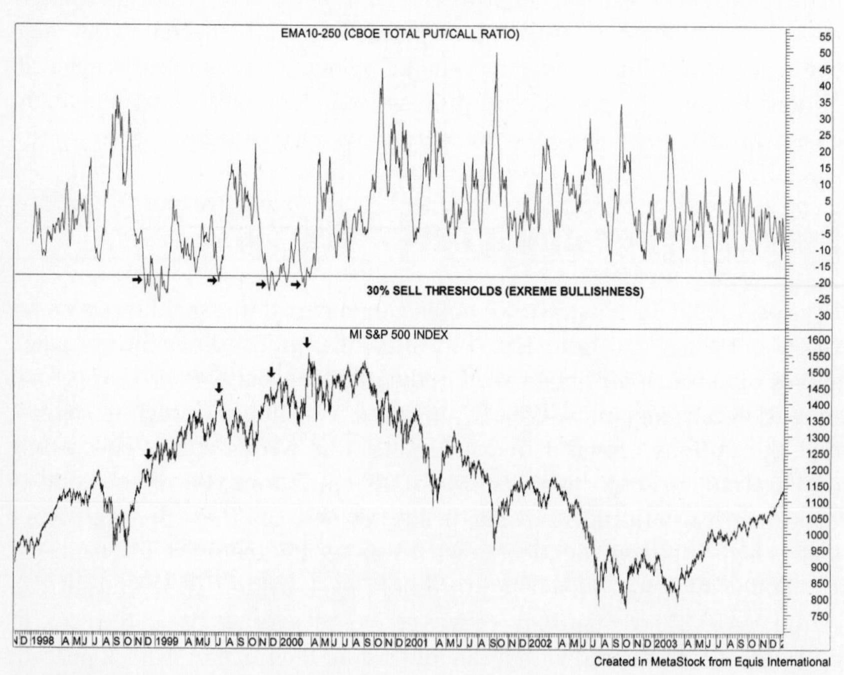

FIGURE 5.2 Extreme bullish thresholds using CBOE total put/call ratio EMA10-250 oscillator. (*Source:* Pinnacle Data.)

TABLE 5.1 Percentage Change in Price of S&P 500 Following Penetration of Extreme Bearish Sentiment Thresholds (CBOE Total Put/Call Ratio EMA10-250 Oscillator)

Sentiment Thresholds	T + 5	T + 10	T + 20	T + 30	T + 40	% Totals
10	5.62	9.79	9.84	11.34	16.96	10.71
15	4.31	8.49	7.75	6.89	11.28	7.74
20	2.01	5.62	6.41	6.37	10.53	6.19
30	1.6	4.02	4.29	3.77	7.37	4.21
40	1.13	2.65	3.01	4.38	8.01	3.84
50	0.35	1.14	2.12	3.83	6.42	2.77
Threshold Average	2.5	5.29	5.57	6.1	10.1	**5.91**
Historical Average	0.1	0.19	0.34	0.44	0.51	**0.32**

Sentiment Thresholds	T + 50	T + 60	T + 120	T + 180	T + 240	% Totals
10	16.36	15.76	18.93	4.82	-9.11	9.35
15	10.37	10.12	8.24	-0.35	-13.02	3.07
20	10.12	9.93	6.75	0.01	-9.86	3.39
30	6.49	6.93	3.35	0.98	-8.35	1.88
40	8.92	9.65	7.65	9.86	5.55	8.33
50	7.18	7.05	5.08	6.62	3.63	5.91
Threshold Average	9.91	9.91	8.33	3.66	-5.19	**5.32**
Historical Average	0.54	0.57	0.54	0.47	-0.22	**0.38**

during the time frames studied. It would appear, therefore, that the presence of index options traders, who tend to be more sophisticated, at the aggregate level do not appear to limit the predictive power of the ratio. Clearly, on average, the numbers are excellent. If we take a subset of this overall data, just the most extreme levels of sentiment (that is, 10 percent, 15 percent, and 20 percent threshold levels) and time frames no longer than T + 40, performance improves significantly: There is a rise from 5.91 percent to 8.21 percent change in price, with a 90.23 percent probability of price rise. (See Tables, 5.1, 5.2 and, 5.3).

TABLE 5.2 Percentage Change in Price of S&P 500 Following Penetration of Extreme Bullish Sentiment Thresholds (CBOE Total Put/Call Ratio EMA10-250 Oscillator)

Thresholds	T + 5	T + 10	T + 20	T + 30	T + 40	Average
10.00	5.62	9.79	9.84	11.34	16.96	10.71
15.00	4.31	8.49	7.75	6.89	11.28	7.74
20.00	2.01	5.62	6.41	6.37	10.53	6.19
Average	3.98	7.97	8.00	8.20	12.92	8.21

Following penetration of the 10 percent buy threshold level, for example, there was an average rise in price of 10.71 percent for the short time frame group, with a probability of the S&P 500 rising 100 percent. As expected, the percentage gains and probabilities decline the further away from the most extreme zones, which conforms to our expectations, as the crowd acts with less unity.

PENETRATION OF EXTREME BULLISH SENTIMENT THRESHOLDS

As for declines in the price of the S&P 500 following penetration of extreme bullish sentiment thresholds, performance was not impressive for this indicator. This may suggest that the index options traders are not as

TABLE 5.3 Probability of a Price Rise Following Penetration of Extreme Bearish Sentiment Thresholds in ≤ T + 30 Time Frames

Thresholds	T + 5	T + 10	T + 20	T + 30	T + 40	Average
10.00	100.00	100.00	100.00	100.00	100.00	100.00
15.00	100.00	100.00	100.00	66.70	66.70	86.68
20.00	60.00	100.00	100.00	80.00	80.00	84.00
Average	86.67	100.00	100.00	82.23	82.23	90.23

likely to get caught up in the herd mentality on Wall Street when the market is overly bullish. At levels of extreme bullishness, we would expect stock market prices to decline over a short- to medium-term horizon, at least by a percentage greater than the historical random average percentage price change during the time frames examined.

The historical random average price change is .38 percent for the S&P 500 over this period, a slightly positive bias. Therefore, to produce reliable market timing values, the expected price changes would need negative values. This indicates actual price declines. In other words, price changes following penetration of extreme bullish sentiment thresholds (that is, too much bullishness by the crowd) should be negative.

Based on this testing method, however, the expected overall price change was a 3.72 percent *rise*, which is the opposite of what the theory of crowd psychology anticipates. A price *fall* does not appear after penetration of extreme bullish thresholds. These options traders were, on average, correct in their trading during bullish periods. If we take a closer look at this performance in terms of shorter versus longer time frames, the longer time frame accounts for most of the correct market sentiment (+3.92 longer time frames versus +.20 for shorter time frames). This shows a slightly worse pattern than with equity-only options traders from a contrary angle.

In Tables 5.4 and 5.5, the very short-term time frames did better. Note how in specific time frames, price changes following penetration of the 10 percent buy threshold level did lead to price declines. The T + 5, T + 10, and T+20 time frames produced average price falls of –2.31 percent, –2.45 percent, and –1.91 percent, respectively, after penetration of the 10 percent threshold levels. The 15 percent threshold produced average price declines in the same time frames too: –.98 percent, –.1.55 percent, and –.88 percent, respectively. This indicates that in very short-term time frames, and after penetration of the most extreme bullish sentiment thresholds, the CBOE total options put/call ratio was reasonably good at forecasting a trend change.

Since the stock market has an historically bullish bias, trading against this tendency would make it inherently more difficult. However, during the sample period of this study (1998–2004), the S&P 500 experienced an almost equal number of bullish and bearish years. As we sift through the data and make some comparisons with the performance of the equity-only put/call ratio, the evidence confirms that the sentiment of equity options traders makes a better indicator.

TABLE 5.4 Percentage Changes in Price of S&P 500 Following Penetration of Extreme Bullish Sentiment Thresholds (CBOE Total Put/Call Ratio EMA10-250 Oscillator)

Sentiment Thresholds	T+5	T+10	T+20	T+30	T+40	% Totals
10	-2.31	-2.45	-1.91	1.13	1.93	-0.72
15	-0.98	-1.55	-0.88	1.43	1.63	-0.07
20	0.18	0.34	1.90	1.95	2.28	1.33
30	0.42	1.08	1.81	1.11	1.53	1.19
40	0.30	0.82	0.67	0.27	0.57	0.53
50	0.05	0.33	-0.01	-0.31	0.00	0.01
Threshold Average	-0.39	-0.24	0.26	0.93	1.32	**0.38**
Historical Average	0.10	0.19	0.34	0.44	0.51	**0.32**

Sentiment Thresholds	T+50	T+60	T+120	T+180	T+240	% Totals
10	1.70	4.95	8.93	2.79	13.09	6.29
15	3.49	4.94	8.13	3.00	12.00	6.31
20	3.24	4.26	7.88	5.47	10.22	6.21
30	2.39	3.16	7.06	4.93	5.96	4.70
40	1.57	2.15	5.30	3.68	3.18	3.18
50	0.82	1.32	4.52	3.56	2.77	2.60
Threshold Average	2.20	3.46	6.97	3.91	7.87	**4.88**
Historical Average	0.54	0.57	0.54	0.47	-0.22	**0.38**

COMPARISON WITH EQUITY-ONLY PUT/CALL RATIO

The sample period covered in this series runs from January 7, 1998 through January 22, 2004, with 1519 days in the sample. It covers almost the identical period used in the equity-only options study in the previous chapter. In terms of overall probability of success during this period, the CBOE total put/call ratio had noticeably less power to predict future price direction, particularly on the downside.

Since index option volume is largely a professional hedging activity, one might expect that the indicator would lose effectiveness with the presence of this professional market sentiment. Indeed, this appears to be the case.

Recall that the theory of contrary opinion is based on the speculative activity of the crowd, not the professional portfolio manager who is interested in hedging stock positions. The performance of the equity-only and CBOE total put/call ratio can be seen in Tables 5.6 and 5.7. In terms of overall average *price change* following extreme bearishness registered in both the indicators under study, the equity-only showed 8.67 percent versus 5.61 percent for the CBOE total put/call ratio, as seen in Table 5.6. Both were good numbers, but clearly the equity traders were better contrarian indicators. In other words, when you throw index options traders into the mix, the reliability of the indicator deteriorates.

TABLE 5.5 Probability of S&P 500 Price Fall Following Penetration of Extreme Bullish Sentiment Thresholds (CBOE Total Put/Call Ratio EMA10-250 Oscillator)

Sentiment Thresholds	T+5	T+10	T+20	T+30	T+40	% Totals
10	100.00	100.00	80.00	40.00	0.00	64.00
15	58.80	76.50	58.80	29.40	17.60	48.22
20	44.10	52.90	32.40	32.40	20.60	36.48
30	37.70	44.20	31.20	44.20	27.30	36.92
40	44.40	44.40	44.40	50.00	39.70	44.58
50	47.40	47.40	49.10	54.90	45.10	48.78
Threshold Average	55.40	60.90	49.32	41.82	25.05	**46.50**
Historical Average	47.2	47.7	45.8	46.6	47	**46.86**
Sentiment Thresholds	**T+50**	**T+60**	**T+120**	**T+180**	**T+240**	**% Totals**
10	20.00	0.00	0.00	20.00	0.00	8.00
15	11.80	11.80	0.00	7.60	5.90	7.42
20	17.60	20.60	2.90	14.70	17.60	14.68
30	24.70	27.30	3.90	22.10	37.70	23.14
40	35.70	33.30	17.50	26.20	43.70	31.28
50	40.60	36.60	22.30	25.10	42.30	33.38
Threshold Average	25.07	21.60	7.77	19.28	24.53	**19.65**
Historical Average	47.2	47.3	52.1	52.5	57.5	**51.32**

TABLE 5.6 Performance Comparison—Extreme Bearish Sentiment Thresholds (Equity-Only versus CBOE Total)

	Equity	Total
% Probability	71.65	72.61
≤ T + 40	77.55	79.83
≥ T + 50	65.76	65.42
% Change	8.67	5.61
≤ T + 40	5.31	5.91
≥ T + 50	12.03	5.32
Expected Change	6.21	4.07
≤ T + 40	4.12	4.72
≥ T + 50	7.91	3.48
Historical S&P	0.18	0.18

Table 5.6 shows the results from penetration of bearish threshold levels (that is, too much bearishness); the equity-only ratio was slightly less, with 71.65 percent versus a 72.61 percent probability of predicting rising price outcomes with CBOE total put/call ratios. In periods that followed extreme bullishness, on the other hand, the equity-only and total put/call ratios were quite close with 2.28 percent and 2.63 percent, respectively, seen in Table 5.7, for average price changes, *both in the wrong direction.* The changes should yield negative, not positive, outcomes. In terms of overall *expected* price changes (which measure the average price change when factoring in the probability of this occurring), the equity-only ratio beats the total put/call ratio by 2.14 percent. As seen in Table 5.7, the equity-only ratio had 6.21 percent expected price change versus 4.07 percent for the CBOE total put/call ratio.

As for penetration of extreme bullish threshold levels, performance probability for both indicators suffers, but with a relatively small drop for the equity-only put/call ratio, which had an overall expected price change of .17 percent versus the historical average of .18 percent. Moreover, the total put/call ratio did even worse, with an overall expected price change of 3.72 percent, a significant *positive* price change after having anticipated a *negative* one. *This tells us that on average, index options traders may be a little better at timing the market than the members of the equity options*

TABLE 5.8 Performance Comparison—Extreme Bullish Sentiment Threshold (Equity-Only versus CBOE Total)

	Equity	CBOE
% Probability	42.48	33.07
≤ T + 40	61.49	46.5
≥ T + 50	23.48	19.65
% Change	2.28	2.63
≤ T + 40	−1.23	0.38
≥ T + 50	3.51	4.88
Expected Change	0.17	3.72
≤ T + 40	−0.47	0.2
≥ T + 50	0.82	3.92
Historical S&P	0.18	0.18

trading crowd, making them less valuable indicators from a contrarian trading perspective.

Taking one look at both of these measures of investor psychology using the most extreme levels of sentiment during short and long time frames separately, the same pattern is visible that is apparent in the aggregate numbers. The CBOE total put/call ratio during ≤ T + 40 time frames had an expected price change of 4.72 percent versus 4.12 percent for the equity-only put call ratio, after extreme bearishness. The equity-only nearly doubles its expected price change in the ≥ T + 50 time frames to 7.91 percent. Meanwhile, the CBOE total put/call ratio expected price change declines to 3.48 percent.

On the opposite extreme of sentiment (too much bullishness), performance patterns for the CBOE total put/call ratio were inferior in both time frames. The equity-only put/call ratio had an expected price change in the shorter time frame group of −.47 while the CBOE total put/call ratio had the wrong expected price change of .20. In the longer time frame group, the equity-only switches signs to .82 and the CBOE total ratio rises to 3.92 percent; both move in the wrong direction based on what is expected if the crowd is systematically wrong at extreme bullish market tops. As I explore the performance of the OEX traders in the next chapter, this same pattern becomes even more pronounced, as the OEX options market appears to contain the smartest traders in the entire options group.

SUMMARY

After looking at the performance of the equity-only options traders as a subgroup of all the options traders in the previous chapter, I examined the performance of both the equity and index traders in the aggregate, as measured in the CBOE total put/call ratio. Data examined in this chapter confirms the long-held belief that when viewed as a group, options traders make good contrarian indicators, even when the so-called smart money is added to the mix. However, the CBOE total put/call ratio is not very reliable at predicting market tops in time frames greater than T + 40, except after the most extreme sentiment zones. Overall performance as a contrarian indicator of market tops was even worse than the equity-only put/call ratio. In the next chapter, I examine a subset of traders in the index options group, who trade the OEX index options.

CHAPTER 6

OEX Options Traders—Is This a Smart Money Crowd?

In this chapter, I examine OEX options trader performance. I evaluate them as a group at moments when they are in conformity about the anticipated direction of the equity markets. The OEX put/call ratio, which represents the sentiment of a subset of index options traders, is applied using the percentage threshold levels analysis applied in the two previous chapters. The results indicate that group sentiment of OEX traders is not a very good indicator for use in trading against the crowd.

Over the years that I have followed put/call ratios, I occasionally noticed that OEX trader sentiment often deviates from that of equity-only options traders, sometimes moving in opposite directions at emotional extremes. The test results presented here confirm my initial suspicion that the OEX index options crowd has transformed into a smart money indicator. According to tests carried out with the same method applied in the two previous chapters, the OEX options trading crowd performed better as a smart money indicator than as an indicator of the wrong-thinking options trading crowd.

As you will see, when the OEX put/call ratio EMA10-250 oscillator moves toward a sentiment extreme, it is often the *correct* sentiment to have (on average) when examining future price changes during both long and short time frames. Therefore, these traders get it *right* more than they get it *wrong*. In practice, this means it is wise to avoid trading against this crowd. However, it might be worthwhile to use the OEX put/call ratio as an indicator to confirm the behavior of the equity-only options trading crowd when it is headed to extremes. Since the OEX put/call ratio appears to move in the opposite direction to the equity-only put/call ratio, it can provide additional information about the health of a market trend. A look at

Figures 6.1 and 6.2, which contain extreme sentiment buy and sell thresholds of the OEX put/call ratio EMA10-250 oscillator, should quickly dispel any notion that the OEX put/call ratio has any value as a measure of the unsophisticated options trading crowd.

While the OEX options traders were certainly not correct at all market turning points, the arrows in Figure 6.1 at market tops correspond closely with penetration of *high* levels of the EMA10-250 put/call ratio oscillator. Recall that put/call ratios of equity-only traders at market tops correspond with *low* levels of put demand relative to call demand (low put/call ratios). Likewise, while there are some exceptions, Figure 6.2 shows the same inverse pattern for market bottoms. When the OEX put/call ratio EMA10-250 oscillator shows a pattern of *low* levels at market bottoms, this indicates more call demand relative to put demand. In other words, OEX options traders appear to be getting it *right*, where the equity-only crowd gets it systematically *wrong*.

It is not clear why the OEX traders are better able to anticipate the future direction of the market. It may have something to do with the migra-

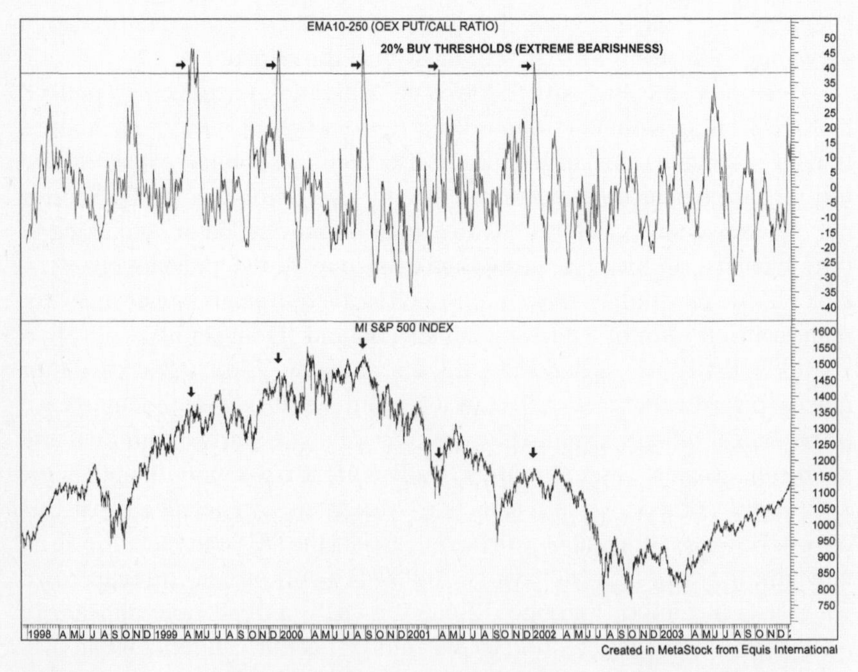

FIGURE 6.1 Extreme bearish sentiment thresholds levels (OEX put/call ratio EMA10-250 oscillator). (*Data Source:* Maridome International)

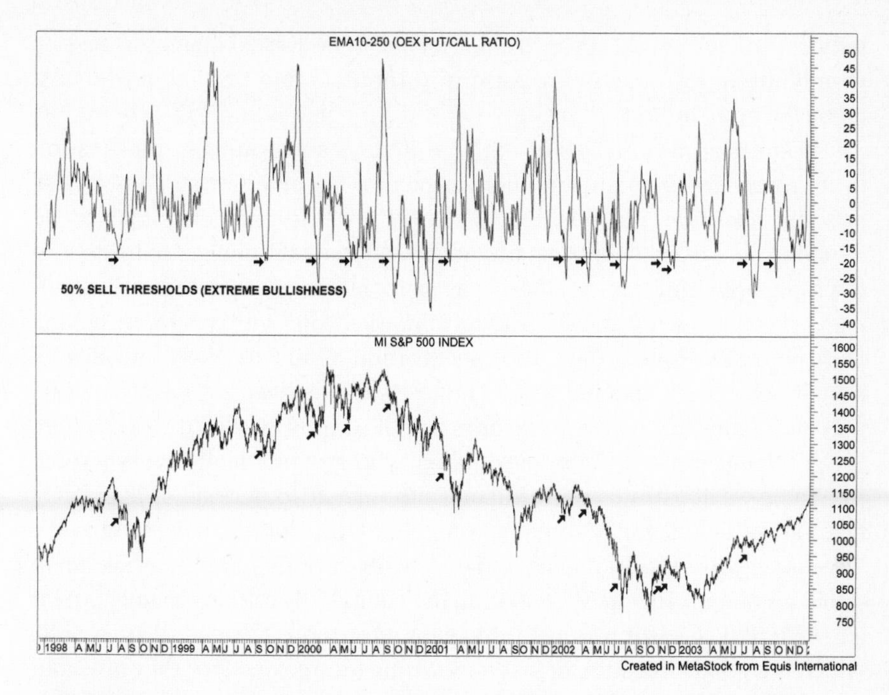

FIGURE 6.2 Extreme bullish sentiment thresholds (OEX put/call ratio EMA10-250 oscillator).

tion of more unsophisticated traders, to options on the QQQs and Diamonds. Although traded on the broad market indices, the latter are counted as equity options, not index options. Perhaps the OEX trading crowd has become relatively more sophisticated, populated by the more professional and seasoned options traders. This is mere conjecture since we do not have any direct proof.

While not all appear perfectly timed, OEX options traders are reliable indicators of trouble ahead for the bulls and bears, but not because they are caught up with the herd. The arrows in Figure 6.1 indicate that the OEX options traders were *correct* at two key market tops, particularly the last failed attempt to run to new highs before the long bear market began its rout of the bulls in early 2000. Even a casual look at this chart should dissuade any astute trader from trading against the OEX options trading crowd. Now let's take a closer look at extreme sentiment thresholds for the OEX put/call ratio EMA10-250 oscillator.

The data series for the OEX put/call ratio EMA10-250 oscillator is longer than for our previous one, so it has even more power in terms of statistical probability. Yet these are not meant to be formal statistical tests. I merely attempt to capture a pattern in the data and provide a practical means of comparison.

In short-term time frames of $\leq T + 40$ days subsequent to penetration of an extremely bearish sentiment zone, the expected price change was actually *negative*, not positive, which is just the opposite of what we would expect from an options trading crowd that is supposed to be getting it wrong, not right. Instead, there was an expected price change of –.4 percent! This suggests that OEX traders at market tops were correctly buying puts, not calls. For the days after penetration of an extremely bullish sentiment zone, the expected price change was positive, not negative (1.05 percent). Once again, this is the opposite of what is desired if OEX traders are good measures of trader psychology who systematically guess wrong.

Table 6.1 illustrates performance subsequent to periods of extremely bearish sentiment for both equity-only and OEX options trading crowds. The data represents the average price gain for each time frame, as shown in the first column. Taking $\leq T + 40$ first, the equity-only options trading crowd shows a 5.31 percent average price gain after their extreme bearish bets, which is a good indication of just how wrong they get it, since they are at an extreme put-buying level and the market on average rises 5.31 percent. Meanwhile, the OEX trading crowd average price change was –.07, a significant difference, and on average, a correct bet. The performance differential increases at the $\geq T + 50$ time frame for average price changes, with the equity-only options-trading crowd's extreme bearishness having an average price gain of 12.03 percent, compared with the OEX options trading crowd's bearishness leading to an average price gain of 2.75 percent. This last figure is less than the random average price gain of 2.80 percent.

In terms of probability and the correct market sentiment, the results, on average, are as follows: The equity-only options trading crowd got it

TABLE 6.1 Equity-Only Versus OEX Put/Call Performance

EMA10-250 Put/Call Oscillator Comparison

	Equity-Only	OEX
Average Price Change (%)		
Time frame $\leq T + 40$	5.31	−0.07
Time frame $\geq T + 50$	12.03	2.75
Probability of Price Rise (%)		
Time frame $\leq T + 40$	77.55	39.29
Time frame $\geq T + 50$	65.76	28.80

wrong 77.55 percent of the time, while the OEX option traders did much better, getting it wrong just 39.29 percent of the time during the shorter time frames. Finally, in the longer time frames, the equity-only options trading crowd got it wrong 65.76 percent of the time, but once again underperformed the OEX traders who were wrong just 28.8 percent of the time.

Upon closer examination, OEX options traders did quite well when they took extreme positions, as seen in Table 6.2. For example, despite the historical bullish bias during the period of this study, which covers the dates February 15, 1985 through January 29, 2004, with 4776 days in the sample, the OEX options traders beat the random historical average price rise of .58 percent in the $\leq$ T + 40 time frames (with an average price change of –.07 for this time frame). These results followed periods when OEX options trader sentiment was extremely bearish. This means that OEX

TABLE 6.2 Percentage Rise in Price of S&P 500 Following Penetration of Extreme Bearish Sentiment Thresholds (OEX Put/Call Ratio EMA10-250 Oscillator)

Sentiment Thresholds	T + 5	T + 10	T + 20	T + 30	T + 40	% Totals
10	–0.64	0.24	–0.99	–1.74	–0.66	–0.76
15	–0.49	0.3	–0.78	–1.41	–0.22	–0.52
20	–0.16	2.78	–0.55	–0.96	0.79	0.38
30	–0.13	0.3	–0.25	–0.57	1.11	0.09
40	0.25	0.33	–0.6	–1.3	0.24	–0.22
50	0.2	0.36	0.46	0.36	1.71	0.62
Threshold Average	–0.16	0.72	–0.45	–0.94	0.5	**–0.07**
Historical Average	0.22	0.33	0.56	0.78	0.99	**0.58**
Sentiment Thresholds	**T + 50**	**T + 60**	**T + 120**	**T + 180**	**T + 240**	**% Totals**
10	1.39	2.81	–0.91	3.41	5.7	2.48
15	1.59	2.84	–1.38	2.13	3.35	1.71
20	2.29	3.12	–0.48	3.14	4.39	2.49
30	2.64	3.25	0.22	4.13	4.84	3.02
40	2.07	2.67	0.39	3.91	3.92	2.59
50	2.78	3.42	2.58	5.81	6.51	4.22
Threshold Average	2.13	3.02	0.07	3.76	4.79	**2.75**
Historical Average	1.2	1.41	2.61	3.86	4.92	**2.8**

options traders were *not excessively bearish* at market bottoms, at least not enough to provide reliable market timing information from a contrarian perspective. When OEX traders were bullish, however, performance was even better throughout these time frames, with an average price change of 1.47 percent. This means that OEX options traders were *not excessively bullish* at market tops, and were to the contrary, positioned to, on average, predict positive price gains of 1.47 percent.

As we move to the longer-term time frames, the bearish bets by OEX traders were not profitable on average, but still came in below the random historical average price change for the S&P 500 of 2.8 percent (versus 2.75 percent for price changes after bearish positions of OEX traders). Finally, in terms of overall probability, the data presented in Table 6.3 show that in short-term time frames the probability of a price rise was just 39.3 percent, and for long-term time frames just 28.8 percent. This indicates that the OEX

TABLE 6.3 Probability of S&P 500 Price Rise at Bearish Thresholds (OEX Put/Call Ratio)

Sentiment Thresholds	T + 5	T + 10	T + 20	T + 30	T + 40	% Totals
10	31.2	40.6	31.2	18.7	34.4	31.22
15	30.9	40.5	28.6	19.1	38.1	31.44
20	38.6	42.1	28.1	26.3	50.9	37.2
30	40	44	30.7	32	56	40.54
40	45.4	47.1	33.9	38.8	54.5	43.94
50	55	49.2	43.9	49.2	59.8	51.42
Threshold Average	40.18	43.92	32.73	30.68	48.95	**39.29**
Historical Average	57.4	58.8	62	63.8	65.89	**61.58**
Sentiment Thresholds	**T + 50**	**T + 60**	**T + 120**	**T + 180**	**T + 240**	**% Totals**
10	46.2	69.2	0	46.2	23.1	36.94
15	26.8	26.8	7.3	14.6	7.3	16.56
20	34.1	31.7	14.6	14.6	12.2	21.44
30	42.4	42.4	18.6	15.3	10.2	25.78
40	43	44.2	30.2	30.2	14	32.32
50	44	46	42.7	40.7	25.3	39.74
Threshold Average	39.42	43.38	18.9	26.93	15.35	**28.8**
Historical Average	67.6	66.5	69.3	70.4	72.5	**69.26**

TABLE 6.4 Percentage Fall in Price of S&P 500 Following Penetration of Extreme Bullish Sentiment Thresholds (OEX Put/Call Ratio EMA10-250 Oscillator)

Sentiment Thresholds	T + 5	T + 10	T + 20	T + 30	T + 40	% Totals
10	−0.38	−0.34	2.22	1.11	0.69	0.66
15	0.81	1.39	1.86	2.44	2.91	1.882
20	0.94	1.58	1.9	2.74	3.4	2.11
30	0.48	0.93	1.92	2.54	3.72	1.92
40	0.33	0.59	0.84	1.63	3.22	1.32
50	0.23	0.32	0.54	1.18	2.31	0.92
Threshold Average	0.4	0.75	1.55	1.94	2.71	**1.47**
Historical Average	0.22	0.33	0.56	0.78	0.99	**0.58**
Sentiment Thresholds	**T + 50**	**T + 60**	**T + 120**	**T + 180**	**T + 240**	**% Totals**
10	3.6	3.58	2.49	6.23	21.53	7.486
15	3.95	5.14	3.49	6.24	22.98	8.36
20	4.17	4.85	3.72	6.27	23.53	8.508
30	3.59	3.64	3.61	8.6	23.58	8.604
40	2.94	2.68	4.91	11.38	22.6	8.902
50	2.55	2.89	6.4	11.9	20	8.748
Threshold Average	3.47	3.8	4.1	8.44	22.37	**8.43**
Historical Average	1.2	1.41	2.61	3.86	4.92	**2.8**

options trading crowd did not get it wrong at market bottoms, and easily beat the random probability of a price rise at any time during the time frames studied, which were 61.6 percent ($\leq$T + 40) and 69.3 percent ($\geq$T + 50). This means that OEX traders were correct in their sentiment when they were buying puts in greater number than calls.

Moreover, as we see in Table 6.4, the bullish bets of the OEX traders, as seen in the $\geq$ T + 50 time frames, had an expected price change of 8.43 percent! Compare this with the historical average price change for the S&P over these time frames of 2.8 percent. The probability of a price fall, furthermore, during the longer time frames was just 13.3 percent when OEX option traders become extremely bullish as shown in Table 6.5. This would make an excellent smart money indicator for picking market bot-

TABLE 6.5 Probability of S&P 500 Price Fall Following Penetration of Extreme Bullish Sentiment Thresholds (OEX Put/Call Ratio EMA10-250 Oscillator)

Sentiment Thresholds	T+5	T+10	T+20	T+30	T+40	% Totals
10	42.2	69.2	0	46.2	23.1	36.14
15	26.8	26.8	7.3	14.6	7.2	16.54
20	34.1	31.7	14.6	14.6	12.2	21.44
30	42.4	42.4	18.6	15.3	10.2	25.78
40	43	44.2	30.2	30.2	14	32.32
50	44	46	42.7	40.7	25.3	39.74
Threshold Average	38.75	43.38	18.9	26.93	15.33	**28.66**
Historical Average	42.6	41.2	38	36.2	34.11	**38.42**

Sentiment Thresholds	T+50	T+60	T+120	T+180	T+240	% Totals
10	0	0	38.5	0	0	7.7
15	0	4.9	29.3	0	0	6.84
20	0	7.3	41.5	2.4	0	10.24
30	10.2	27.1	39	1.7	0	15.6
40	17.4	37.2	34.9	3.5	2.3	19.06
50	21.3	31.3	29.3	10.7	9.3	20.38
Threshold Average	8.15	17.97	35.42	3.05	1.93	**13.3**
Historical Average	32.4	33.5	30.7	29.6	27.5	**30.74**

toms. Clearly, when the OEX traders are in conformity in their call buying, they are not, on average, getting it wrong.

COMPARISON WITH EQUITY-ONLY PUT/CALL RATIO

How does this compare with the equity-only put/call ratio? In the shorter-term time frames after bullish bets by equity-only option traders, the S&P 500 fell on average by –1.23 percent. However, over longer-term time frames, the S&P 500 average price changes on these extremely bullish days were associated with a rise 3.51 percent, significantly below the 8.42 percent price rise registered by OEX traders when they are overly bullish. Although the OEX sample period covers a longer time span creating an imperfect comparison, there is clearly a differential rate of performance.

SUMMARY

From the data analyzed in this chapter, there appears to be a relatively more sophisticated trading crowd amidst OEX index options traders. OEX options traders on average were more correct than equity-only options traders during bullish and bearish sentiment extremes. While OEX traders did not always get it right, there is enough evidence here to suggest that they are generally good at timing the market. While it is still a common practice in the business press to refer to OEX put/call ratios as measures of the options trading crowd, traders should avoid trading against this crowd, and may find it more profitable to trade with these options traders.

CHAPTER 7

From Statistical Tests to Sentiment Trading System

In the preceding chapters, some simple statistical analysis confirmed that total and equity-only put/call ratios not only reflect investor and trader sentiment, but that at extremes they indicate how *wrong* that sentiment can be among the investing and trading crowd. Since equity-only traders on average were the best indicators of common misjudgments made by the crowd, this chapter attempts to build a trading system out of this apparent market inefficiency. After custom indicators are constructed and used in the trading systems in this chapter, I modify and apply them in future chapters when covering other sentiment data series, such as implied volatility, public short sales data, advisory opinion, and my own bear-and-bull news flow intensity indices.

BUILDING CUSTOM INDICATORS

The custom indicators I present here process raw put/call ratio data into smoothed oscillators, similar to the EMA10-250 oscillator used in the previous chapter tests. I use two custom indicators for the system presented in this chapter. The first is an oscillator that is derived by differencing the 5- and 21-day exponential moving averages (EMA5-21). The second custom indicator (EMA21-50) also is an oscillator, but it uses the 21-day exponential moving average as the faster, smoothed series; and a slower series, a 50-day exponential moving average. The MetaStock and TradeStation code for these custom indicators can be found in Appendix A at the back of this book.

The trading system, which I call Squeeze Play I, incorporates the equity-only put/call ratio into oscillators just mentioned. There are, thus, two time frames of option sentiment utilized, a short-term oscillator (EMA5-21), which will be used to time entries, and a medium-term oscillator (EMA21-50) used to get out of trades. The system rules for Squeeze Play I are presented in Table 7.1.

At this stage, I am not using a price-based trigger with the sentiment oscillators; I add those in the following chapter. The system works like this: When the EMA5-21 oscillator moves from an excessively bullish zone (defined as moving *from above to below* zero), a long trade is entered. Likewise, when the EMA5-21 moves *from below to above* zero, a short trade is entered. The wavelike pattern of the short- and medium-term oscillators can be viewed in Figure 7.1.

Now that I have our entry strategy, a mechanical exit rule is needed. I have found the exit strategy to be the Achilles heel of most trading systems. In other words, it is often easy to find good entries, but the system performance suffers largely due to pure timing of exits.

On the exit side of the system, long trades are closed when the EPC21-50 itself crosses *from above to below* the zero-level threshold (average sentiment), and short trades are closed when the EPC21-50 crosses *from below to above* the zero-level threshold (average sentiment).

Many traders work with trailing stops, profit targets, maximum loss stops, or a combination of these along with money management (that is, how large a position to take on entry, and how much to take off the table at specified exit targets). The process can be frustrating and often requires

TABLE 7.1 Squeeze Play I Trading System Rules (No Price Trigger)

Long Entry Signal	Short Entry Signal
Enter a long position on tomorrow's open when **EMA5-21** has crossed on a closing basis from *above* zero to *below* zero.	Enter a short position on tomorrow's open when **EMA5-21** has crossed on a closing basis from *below* zero to *above* zero.
Long Exit Signal	**Short Exit Signal**
Exit long position on tomorrow's open when **EPC21-50** has crossed on a closing basis from *above* zero to *below* zero.	Exit short position on tomorrow's open when **EPC21-50** has crossed on a closing basis from *below* zero to *above* zero.

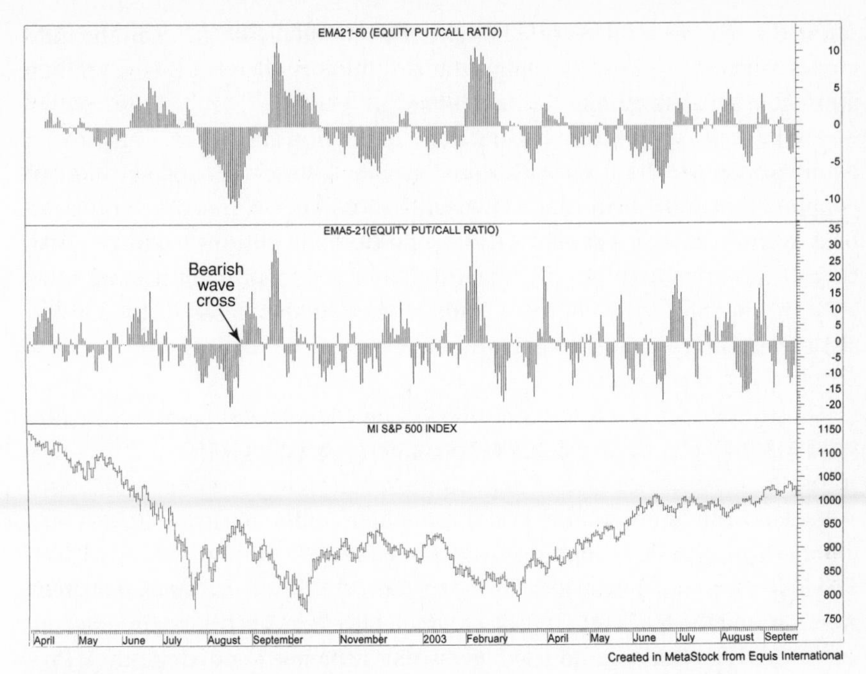

FIGURE 7.1 EMA5-21 and EMA21-50 oscillator waves and S&P 500.

system optimization to find the best approach, which hardly leaves me feeling confident about the results. I prefer to avoid trying to find just the right stop loss or trailing stop loss parameters. Therefore, for now I operate without any stop loss management. Use of stop losses is addressed later in this book.

Optimization is used in this book. However, while I do run optimization routines, the aim is *not* to find the best fit, but to see if the optimization results *indicate a robust system*. That is, does the system make money across most or all optimization parameters, and are those results relatively uniform? Or, does the profitability depend on a few parameters, or even a single one? Clearly, it is important to find systems that profit on as many parameter values as possible.

One of the problems typically encountered using sentiment data on its own is that entries are often too early, which is common with all market-timing approaches that try to identify overbought and oversold levels. Too often, the market remains overbought or oversold far longer than the indicators suggest, seriously eroding the profitability of most swing trading approaches, causing painful drawdowns.

In light of results from testing done in previous chapters, I employ an equity-only put/call ratio series in the system tests in this and subsequent chapters that address the use of put/call ratios, since it appears to offer the best overall value as a gauge of the wrong-thinking options trading crowd. Using this series first, I apply Squeeze Play I with sentiment trading rules only. In a second round of tests, I add a price trigger to see if there is any significant improvement in performance.

SQUEEZE PLAY I PERFORMANCE ANALYSIS

To begin, I run Squeeze Play I on three major equity market averages during a six-year period, running from January 1997 through January 2004. The following equity cash indices are tested: S&P 500, Dow Jones Industrial Average, and the NASDAQ 100, all of which have actively traded futures contracts or ETFs that can be used as trading vehicles. I use MetaStock Professional for backtesting (see Appendices A and B for system code in TradeStation and MetaStock formula languages).

This system, and those presented later, can be traded with futures or ETFs on the equity indices. However, these tests are conducted on the cash indices. The Squeeze Play I system code is simple to understand, and can easily be reproduced. For entries and exits, there is one price delay, which means that, following a signal generation at the close of a trading day, for example, the system enters a trade at the market opening on the following day. The exact dates for the back tests are provided in the tables that contain the results for each market.

As you can see in Table 7.2, results are mixed for Squeeze Play I using the EMA5-21 oscillator without a price trigger. Long trades do better than short trades, but overall performance is not acceptable even though a profit is shown. Total net profit was 312.7 cash index points (worth $250 each), with a maximum open system drawdown of –74.4 points (but an open trade drawdown of –286.1 points).

The buy/hold index is –1.98, which tells us that the system did not produce more net profit than the buy/hold profit of 406.8 points. This is a critical assessment variable for any trading system, since it might not be worth all the effort if the buy/hold profit rate is superior to the trading system. The

TABLE 7.2 Squeeze Play I Trading System Performance (No Price Trigger) for S&P 500 (1/02/97–1/22/04)

Squeeze Play I (EMA5-21) Points-Only Test on CBOE Equity Put/Call Ratio

Total net profit	312.69		
Buy/Hold profit	406.88	Average length of loss	36.25
Days in test	2577	Longest winning trade	88
Total closed trades	41	Longest losing trade	68
		Most consecutive wins	9
		Most consecutive losses	3
Average profit per trade	5.53	Total bars out	623
Average Win/Average Loss ratio	0.56	Average length out	14.83
Total long trades	41		
Total winning trades	29	Longest out period	47
Total losing trades	12		
		System close drawdown	0.00
		Profit/Loss index	32.29
Amount of winning trades	882.32	System open drawdown	–74.44
Amount of losing trades	–655.75		
Average win	30.42	Reward/Risk index	80.77
Average loss	–54.65		
Largest win	149.21	Maximum open trade drawdown	–286.10
		Buy/Hold index	–1.98
Average length of win	26.52		

system will need to do better than this before committing real money to the markets based on opinions of the options trading crowd. Several additional key performance numbers also were not appealing. For example, average loss exceeds average wins, –54.65 versus 30.42 points.

Tables 7.3 and 7.4 show that the substitution of slower sentiment waves/oscillators EMA21-50 and EMA50-250 for sentiment screens, given the same exit plan, did not improve performance. Instead there is a decline of total net profit from 312.7 index points to 151 points when we substitute the EMA21-50 for the EMA5-21 in the system test. Moreover, when the slower EMA50-250 custom indicator is used, a positive total net profit now becomes a net loss of –127.5 cash index points. The slower EMA50-250, moreover, was very poor in most of the essential test performance variables, most notably having an open system drawdown of –669.5 points.

TABLE 7.3 Squeeze Play I Trading System Performance (No Price Trigger) for S&P 500 using an EMA21-50 oscillator (1/02/97–1/22/04)

Squeeze Play I (EMA21-50) Points-Only Test on CBOE Equity Put/Call Ratio			
Total net profit	151.00	Average length of win	22.79
Buy/Hold profit	406.8800	Average length of loss	6.29
		Longest winning trade	173
Days in test	2577	Longest losing trade	29
Total closed trades	36	Most consecutive wins	4
Average profit per trade	0.98	Most consecutive losses	3
		Total bars out	1214
Average Win/Average Loss ratio	0.99	Average length out	32.81
Total long trades	36		
Total winning trades	19	Longest out period	97
Total losing trades	17		
		System close drawdown	–47.55
Amount of winning trades	359.41	Profit/Loss index	31.80
Amount of losing trades	–324.23	System open drawdown	–55.41
Average win	18.92	Reward/Risk index	73.18
Average loss	–19.07	Maximum open trade drawdown	–90.88
Largest win	125.81		
Largest loss	–51.51	Buy/Hold index	34.34

TABLE 7.4 Squeeze Play I Trading System Performance (No Price Trigger) for S&P 500 Using an EMA50-250 Oscillator (1/02/97–1/22/04)

Squeeze Play I (EMA50-250) Points-Only Test on CBOE Equity Put/Call Ratio			
Total net profit	–127.49	Average length of win	62.75
Buy/Hold profit	406.88	Average length of loss	328.00
		Longest winning trade	199
Days in test	2577	Longest losing trade	650
Total closed trades	6	Most consecutive wins	3
		Most consecutive losses	2
Average profit per trade	–48.5133	Total bars out	770
Average Win/Average Loss ratio	0.23		
Total long trades	6	Longest out period	305
Total winning trades	4		
Total losing trades	2	System close drawdown	–394.67
		Profit/Loss index	–33.90
Amount of winning trades	248.63	System open drawdown	–538.66
		Reward/Risk index	–23.67
Amount of losing trades	–539.71		
Average win	62.16	Maximum open trade drawdown	–669.53
Average loss	–269.85		
Largest win	145.04		
Largest loss	–525.54	Buy/Hold index	–91.13

SUMMARY

This chapter presents results from a preliminary investor sentiment trading system setup, which does not contain price-based triggers or stop losses. The CBOE equity-only option put/call ratio was used for a measure of options trading crowd sentiment in the system tests. An EMA5-21 oscillator was used as an entry screen. Performance of the tests using EMA5-21, as well as EMA21-50 and EMA50-250 oscillators, failed to produce viable results. In the next chapter, I introduce a basic price-based entry trigger mechanism, which is added to the Squeeze Play I system rules outlined in this chapter. I use price-based filters for trade entries and the EMA5-21 sentiment oscillator screen as an initial screening mechanism. Let's see if performance can be improved to an acceptable level for risking real money.

CHAPTER 8

Squeeze Play I: Pulling the Price Trigger

The Squeeze Play I option sentiment trading system explored in the previous chapter allows trade entry, either long or short, if the EMA5-21 oscillator value has been above zero (longs) or below zero (shorts), and then experiences a crossover. Just to reiterate what is happening during this crossover, when the oscillator crosses to the negative, the options trading crowd moves from a previously bearish mood to a bullish state. This is captured in the faster-moving EMA5-21 oscillator, so the hope is that it catches the start of a sentiment reversal. The presumption is that sentiment is experiencing a sudden change, from what were excessive levels before the cross. At this point, there is no specification in the system code to require any specific prior level of extreme sentiment. The sentiment measured in the EMA5-21 oscillator just needs to have been above average levels of sentiment, then suddenly to have reversed to get us into the trade. As for exits, when the slower (EMA21-50) oscillator follows this path, it is time to get out.

Why should this work? Admittedly, this is a crude approach, but on average, it has the possibility to catch sentiment reversals. To improve the hit rate, in this chapter I add an important, yet simple, price-based trigger to the equation. As seen in Table 8.1, the entry rule for long positions now includes a close above the high of the previous day by the cash index price. For short positions, a close below the low of the previous day is required. The logic behind this price trigger rule is the idea of a "squeeze," hence the term Squeeze Play. Price action catches the majority by surprise.

For many years, I have experimented with trading systems, and know how hard it is to find a reliable one, which meets all my expectations. Since I am not a computer programmer, I have always had to keep my programming language simple which, at the end of the day, often yields the best

TABLE 8.1 Squeeze Play I System Rules with Price Trigger

Long Entry Signal	Short Entry Signal
Rule #1: Enter a long position on tomorrow's open when **EMA5-21** has crossed on a closing basis *from above to below* zero.	*Rule #1:* Enter a short position on tomorrow's open when **EMA5-21** has crossed on a closing basis *from below to above* zero.
Rule #2: Enter a long position if today's close is *greater* than the previous day's *high*.	*Rule #2:* Enter a short position if today's close is *less* than the previous day's *low*.
Long Exit Signal	**Short Exit Signal**
Exit a long position on tomorrow's open when **EPC21-50** has crossed on a closing basis *from above to below* zero.	Exit a short position on tomorrow's open when **EPC21-50** has crossed on a closing basis *from below to above* zero.

results. I am a big believer in the KISS (Keep It Simple, Stupid) philosophy. This applies as much to my trading systems development and testing as it does in my money management techniques and my personal life.

One basic setup that has been a favorite of mine is a short-term variation of the simple price breakout method. Long-term trend followers like to go long when market price breaks out above the high of a previous number of days (typically a 20-day high). My price-triggered Squeeze Play I system trades in much shorter time frames, using a much tighter range, using a close above the previous day's high or below the low as the trigger.

Using a closing value instead of an intraday price move, I avoid what are often false moves arising from market noise that can often trigger buy stops and sell stops intraday just before reversing. Since I am looking for a solid confirmation of an impending move up or down, I want a close *above or below* the previous day's high or low, respectively.

TESTING SQUEEZE PLAY I WITH A PRICE TRIGGER

I add the basic price trigger to the system tested in the previous chapter and rerun tests on the S&P 500. Following tests on the S&P 500, I run the system on other major market averages to evaluate just how robust Squeeze

Play I is with a price trigger. Following these tests, I modify this price trigger parameter setting to evaluate how reliable the triggers are across multiple parameter values. Finally, there are no traditional price-based stops used. Instead, the system reverses when the EMA5-21 recrosses the average (zero) line, in effect limiting losses.

The addition of a price trigger shows significant improvement in Squeeze Play I performance. As you can see from the test results presented in Table 8.2, a simple trigger mechanism makes a critical difference. All test dates cover the period January 2, 1997 through January 22, 2004. Running Squeeze Play I with the simple price trigger beginning with longs only, the system improves substantially. There are now reasonably good results on the key performance statistics. Total net profit (643.47 points) easily beat the buy-and-hold profit (406.88). This is a necessary first condition for a good trading system. Next, an average win increased to 40.49 points, while an average loss was just −17.31, an excellent average buy/loss spread. This is even more impressive given the fact that the percentage of winners was 68 percent with 17 winners and 8 losers. This is particularly good given the

TABLE 8.2 EMA5-21 Squeeze Play I with Basic Price Trigger—S&P 500 (Longs Only)

Total net profit	643.47	Average length of win	32.24
		Average length of loss	30.38
Buy/Hold profit	406.88	Longest winning trade	88
		Longest losing trade	68
Days in test	2577	Most consecutive wins	4
Total closed trades	25	Most consecutive losses	2
		Total bars out	997
Average profit per trade	21.9896	Average length out	38.35
Average Win/Average Loss ratio	2.34	Longest out period	127
Total long trades	25		
Winning long trades	17	System close drawdown	0.0
Total losing trades	8	Profit/Loss index	82.29
Amount of winning trades	688.27	System open drawdown	−282.40
Amount of losing trades	−138.53	Reward/Risk index	89.63
Average win	40.49		
Average loss	−17.31	Maximum open trade	
Largest win	149.21	drawdown	−223.57
Largest loss	−73.12	Buy/Hold index	81.18

closed system drawdown of zero. There is still a high open trade drawdown of –223.6 points, but the largest closed trade loss experienced was –73 points.

Furthermore, there is an excellent reward/risk index number of 89.63, which compares the *amount* of winning trades to the *amount* of losing trades (100 is maximum performance). Also the profit/loss index is 82.29 (out of a perfect 100), which combines winning trades and losing trades into one value (–100 is the worst and 100 is the best).

When the profit/loss index has no losing trades, for example, the index would be 100, and when it has no winning trades, it is at –100. Therefore, a profit/loss index of 82.29 is a very good score, with 688.27 winning points compared with –138.53 losing points.

The net profit is higher than total winning minus losing points would indicate because the last trade was not closed by the system during the test, leaving an unrealized gain of nearly 100 points on the position. The last trade in the system test was entered on November 25, 2003, at which point there were 549.74 winning points gained. As of January 22, 2004, this trade was still open with a total net profit on the system of 643.47 (shown in Table 8.2). Since the trade was not closed, however, this additional gain is *not* reflected in the total winning trades column, but it *is* shown in total net profits. The trade needs to be closed to be counted in the profit/loss performance field.

LONGS AND SHORTS COMBINED

Performance improves further when we go to a combined long and short system, as was tested in the previous chapter. Recall that Squeeze Play I without a price trigger generated just 312 points in profit and did not beat the buy-and-hold number. The test results presented in Table 8.3 now show a dramatic improvement. Total net profit jumps to 763.71 index points, which nearly doubles the buy-and-hold profit of 406.88. Meanwhile, the open system drawdown falls to –54.23 and the maximum open trade drawdown decreases to –128.19 (reflecting reversal trades that cut losses short). An average win was 40.53 points compared with an average loss of –26.37. The ratio of wins to losses was 1.54, which is a very good number.

In a test run of a shorts-only Squeeze Play I system there was a substantial loss of over 400 points using the non-trigger test (not shown), though there was a net loss of just –19.29 points with a trigger added, as seen in Table 8.4. While the shorts-only is not impressive on its own, clearly

TABLE 8.3 EMA5-21 Squeeze Play I with Basic Price Trigger—S&P 500 (Longs/Shorts)

Total net profit	763.71	Largest win	120.60
Buy/Hold profit	406.88	Largest loss	−109.28
		Average length of win	15.37
Days in test	2577	Average length of loss	15.73
Total closed trades	71	Longest winning trade	42
		Longest losing trade	68
Average Win/Average Loss ratio	1.54	Total bars out	744
Total long trades	37	Longest out period	69
Total short trades	34		
Winning long trades	21	System close drawdown	−22.53
Winning short trades	17		
Total winning trades	38	Profit/Loss index	46.74
Total losing trades	33	System open drawdown	−54.23
		Reward/Risk index	93.37
Amount of winning trades	1540.20		
Amount of losing trades	−870.22	Maximum open trade drawdown	−128.19
Average win	40.53		
Average loss	−26.37	Buy/Hold index	110.74

Source: Created using MetaStock Professional from Equis International.

TABLE 8.4 EMA5-21 Squeeze Play I with Basic Price Trigger—S&P 500 (Shorts Only)

Total net profit	−19.29	Average length of win	19.36
Buy/Hold profit	406.88	Average length of loss	46.36
		Longest winning trade	50
Days in test	2577	Longest losing trade	108
Total closed trades	25	Most consecutive wins	4
		Most consecutive losses	3
Average profit per trade	3.79	Total bars out	1004
		Average length out	38.62
Average Win/Average Loss ratio	0.95		
Total short trades	25	Longest out period	118
Winning short trades	14		
Total losing trades	11	System close drawdown	−195.45
		Profit/Loss index	−3.34
Amount of winning trades	557.97	System open drawdown	−282.40
		Reward/Risk index	−6.83
Amount of losing trades	−463.29		
Average win	39.855	Maximum open trade drawdown	
Average loss	−42.12		−170.76
Largest win	120.6	Buy/Hold index	−132.75
Largest loss	−135.21		

Source: Created using MetaStock Professional from Equis International.

there is a synergy when shorts and longs are combined that allows for the improved results seen in the long/short tests presented in Table 8.3.

Adding a proprietary sentiment filter to the Squeeze Play I setup, finally, I ran the test again, and the results are presented in Table 8.5. Total net profit jumps to 1141.4 index points, with the maximum open trade drawdown falling to –83.36 and system open drawdown showing just –24.48 points. An average win is 32.65, lower than without the proprietary filter, but average loss is lower, too, at –13.58, leaving a win/loss profit ratio of 2.4. It does not get much better than this. Figure 8.1 contains the equity growth for this system testing time frame, which is quite stable.

When applied to the other major equity indices, results were equally good. The results are summarized in Table 8.6. If these systems were traded with equity index futures, the total percentage gains for the period studied would have been 951, 900, and 1,222 percent, respectively, for the S&P 500, Dow Jones Industrial Average, and NASDAQ 100. Total net dollar profit was $285,350 (S&P 500), $90,032 (DJIA), and $183,314 (NASDAQ

TABLE 8.5 EMA5-21 Squeeze Play I with Basic Price Trigger/Secondary Proprietary Screen—S&P 500 (Longs/Shorts)

Total net profit	1141.40	Largest win	120.60
Buy/Hold profit	406.88		
		Largest loss	–26.80
Days in test	2577		
Total closed trades	42	Average length of win	15.40
		Average length of loss	12.29
Average profit per trade	24.9445	Longest winning trade	55
		Longest losing trade	26
Average Win/Average Loss ratio	2.40	Most consecutive wins	13
Total long trades	22	Most consecutive losses	1
Total short trades	20	Total bars out	1193
Winning long trades	19	Longest out period	114
Winning short trades	16		
Total winning trades	35	System close drawdown	0.00
Total losing trades	7	Profit/Loss index	92.31
		System open drawdown	–24.48
Amount of winning trades	1142.73	Reward/Risk index	97.90
Amount of losing trades	–95.06	Maximum open trade	
Average win	32.65	drawdown	–83.36
Average loss	–13.58	Buy/Hold index	203.56

Source: Created using MetaStock Professional from Equis International.

FIGURE 8.1 Equity growth for Squeeze Play I with proprietary filter and triggers on S&P 500. *Data Source:* Pinnacle Data.

100). The initial account starting balances for each market were $30,000, $10,000, and $15,000, respectively. As Table 8.6 clearly shows, the buy and hold approaches are exceeded substantially. The S&P 500 tests, for example, produced over $180,000 in net profit above the buy-and-hold profit.

TABLE 8.6 Squeeze Play I Percentage Gain/Loss for S&P 500, DJIA, and NASDAQ Using Equity Index Futures Contracts (Jan 2, 1997–Jan 22, 2004

Squeeze Play I: Summary of Performance

Futures Market	Net Profit ($)	Buy/Hold Profit ($)	Initial Account Size ($)	Gain/Loss (%)
S&P 500	285,350	101,720	30,000	951
DJIA	90,032	41,620	10,000	900
NASDAQ	183,314	7,875	15,000	1,222

Data Source: Summa Capital Management & Research.

TABLE 8.7 EMA5-21 Squeeze Play I with Basic Price Trigger with (Long/Short) on OEX Cash Index

Total net profit	423.54	Largest win	68.33
Buy/Hold profit	208.65	Largest loss	–44.49
Days in test	2577	Average length of win	17.85
Total closed trades	73	Average length of loss	10.06
		Longest winning trade	46
Average profit per trade	5.13	Longest losing trade	40
		Most consecutive wins	7
Average Win/Average Loss ratio	1.57	Most consecutive losses	5
Total long trades	39	Total bars out	805
Total short trades	34	Longest out period	69
Winning long trades	22		
Winning short trades	18	System close drawdown	–12.24
Total winning trades	40	Profit/Loss index	50.66
Total losing trades	33	System open drawdown	–29.32
		Reward/Risk index	93.52
Amount of winning trades	786.92		
Amount of losing trades	–412.48	Maximum open trade drawdown	–67.18
Average win	19.67		
Average loss	–12.50	Buy/Hold index	126.53

Source: Created using MetaStock Professional from Equis International.

APPLYING SQUEEZE PLAY I TO THE OEX

In Table 8.7, performance results for testing on the S&P 100 (OEX) stock index, a popular index option for traders, is presented. Squeeze Play I did well on the OEX, with a total net profit of 423.54 points compared to a buy-and-hold profit of 208.65. The system close drawdown was just –12.24 points. The average-win-to-average-loss ratio was 1.57, with a ratio of winners to losers greater than 50 percent. Finally the reward/risk index of 93 suggests that this system offers as much promise as when applied to the other major market averages covered above.

SUMMARY

This chapter demonstrates how adding a price trigger to Squeeze Play I produced substantial improvement in the use of equity-only put/call ratios as a measure of the unsophisticated options trader sentiment. First applied to the S&P 500, the system was then run on the Dow Jones Industrial Average and NASDAQ 100 (without optimization), and finally the OEX S&P 100 equity index. Performance was quite consistent across each of these equity indices. Calculating dollar rates of return using futures contracts, gains were highest (1,222 percent) on the NASDAQ 100 for the seven-year period of the test and the lowest on the DJIA (900 percent). Total return on the S&P 500 futures contract was 951 percent for the period. The average annual gain for the three contracts combined was 146.3 percent. The tests did not include commissions and slippage, but given the small number of trades and the type of position trading employed, this would have had only a minor impact on performance. Later, in tests that take many more trades, I factor commission costs into the performance results.

CHAPTER 9

Sentiment Squeeze Play II

With the excellent results achieved in the previous chapter using Squeeze Play I with price triggers on stock indices, it would make sense to extend such a system to individual stocks to see if similar profitable performance can be achieved. After all, stock indices are merely aggregates of individual stock prices, and aggregate equity-only put/call ratios are taken from individual stock options volume each day. Logically therefore, individual stocks should be an excellent place to apply such crowd psychology gauges. However, a preliminary assessment of the data indicates that there is too much noise using the EMA5-21 oscillator on individual stock options put/call ratios. As a result, Squeeze Play I needs to be modified. I call this new system Squeeze Play II.

Many big-cap stocks today—whether "new economy" tech stocks like Microsoft (MSFT) or old-style, brick-and-mortar companies like General Electric (GE)—have actively traded listed options, which offer an excellent secondary data stream for gauging market sentiment.

A look at the most active puts and calls at the Chicago Board of Trade (CBOT) for April 9, 2004 offers a glimpse of the nature of the listed stock options market, with its mix of options traded on stocks, stock indices, and exchange traded funds (ETFs). As you can see in Figures 9.1 and 9.2, the volume can top 5,000 on a daily basis for some of the most active option contracts. For example, Figure 9.1 shows that on this particular day, Microsoft had the lead stock option call contract. The August 30 strike traded 5,965 contracts, with a last sale of 35¢. For puts, as seen in Figure 9.2, Proctor & Gamble (PG) had the leading stock options contract.

Some options traders monitor daily stock options volume in relation to open interest on individual stocks in order to find potential big movers, with the assumption that the smart money must know something. This is presumably why the volume in put options or call options series is sometimes inexplicably on the rise. This assumes, of course, that there is no

	SERIES	VOLUME	LAST SALE	CHANGE
SPQ AM	AUG 1075	7,787	49.00	- .60
OEX D	JUL 545	7,099	2.35	- .15
QQQ	DEC 35	6,806	2.80	- .10
QQQ	DEC 38	6,804	1.25	- .10
QQQ	DEC 40	6,800	.70	- .10
S P T	JUL 1125	6,454	1.90	- .80
MSFT	AUG 30	5,965	.35	+ .05
MSFT	JUL 27 1/2	5,375	.60	+ .10
ASML	AUG 17 1/2	5,030	.35	- .30
APPX	OCT 20	5,000	6.30	- 18.40
ASML	JUL 17 1/2	5,000	.05	- .05
WM 06	JAN 40	5,000	3.00	
QQQ	JUL 35	4,581	.70	- .20
DJX O	JUL 103	4,189	.25	
S P T	AUG 1125	4,098	15.00	+ .10
EMC	OCT 11	4,077	.80	+ .10
OEX D	JUL 550	3,949	.75	- .20
OEX D	JUL 540	3,653	5.40	
MSFT	AUG 27 1/2	3,537	1.20	
FLML	DEC 15	3,500	7.20	- .10

FIGURE 9.1 Most active CBOE call options series. (*Source:* CBOE.)

pending news about a stock. Without an obvious reason, extra volume may be attributable to insider speculation on the likely direction of the stock in anticipation of an impending news announcement or company development.

But this "noise" in the markets only causes trouble for put/call ratios, since we are looking for prolonged sentiment waves, either bullish or bearish, that provide a reliable setup for entering a trade using price triggers. To clarify, the emphasis is almost exclusively on what the "dumb" (unso-

	SERIES	VOLUME	LAST SALE	CHANGE
QQQ	JUL 36	36,236	.60	+ .10
QQQ	JUL 37	27,673	1.40	+ .15
NDX B	AUG 1275	12,953	6.10	+ .90
NDX B	AUG 1250	12,642	3.80	- .60
NDX B	JUL 1325	12,605	.50	+ .25
NDX B	JUL 1350	12,579	.40	- .45
IWM A	JUL 109	10,374	.25	- .05
WM 07	JAN 30	10,010	2.35	+ .20
PG 06	JAN 55	9,136	4.30	+ .70
S P T	SEP 1100	8,195	24.20	- 2.10
S P T	JUL 1100	7,399	2.45	- .75
SPQ AM	JUL 1050	7,098	.20	- .10
QQQ A	DEC 31	6,800	.90	+ .20
OEX D	JUL 540	5,922	1.75	- .85
SPQ AM	AUG 1050	5,912	5.50	- .60
DIA	AUG 100	5,888	1.00	- .10
OEX D	JUL 545	5,680	3.90	- 1.00
AMR 06	JAN 10	5,500	3.70	
S P T	JUL 1110	5,166	4.60	- 1.80
AMR	JAN 7 1/2	5,000	1.20	+ .20

FIGURE 9.2 Most active CBOE put options series. (*Source:* CBOE.)

phisticated) money is doing. Remember, we want to look for sentiment extremes, when markets are most predictable, and then find a timely entry point. And one day's activity does not provide sufficient information about the crowd's mood.

My approach, therefore, is not to try to predict if and when a stock is about to explode in one direction or another based on what the "smart" money might be buying in the listed options market. I am not suggesting that this approach is not effective. I have no way to know since I have never evaluated it. I simply want to distinguish it from the approach to trading stocks employed here. We are taking positions based on what the smoothed put/call ratio oscillators are telling us about the prevailing sentiment in the market. These indicators tell us if the crowd has turned too greedy or too fearful as reflected in the ratio of the daily volume of puts or calls being purchased (on average).

Let's begin to examine the raw data. The CBOE average daily options volume for May 2004 is presented in Table 9.3. Leading the group is Microsoft, with 355,059 call options and 219,264 put options traded. The average daily volume (ADV) is shown as well, with 16,908 for calls and 10,441 for puts. A put/call ratio can be calculated using these 21-day average daily volumes (ADV). By dividing 10,441 (put ADV) by 16,908 (put ADV), the put/call ratio is .548. However, this approach for deriving ratios does not work for my purpose. I need a historical series that can be constructed easily from the raw *daily* numbers and manipulated into different moving average speeds. So the exchange data offers limited use; however, it does provide a glimpse of leaders in this market and average daily volumes for illustrative purposes.

EMA50-100 SQUEEZE PLAY II

Turning to system testing, I have somewhat randomly selected a group of stocks from different industries to use as a sample, with the stocks having only one feature in common—they are big-cap stocks with actively traded options. Among the sample of six, IBM, MSFT, GE, Wal-Mart, and Citigroup are seen among the volume leaders, shown in Figure 9.3. The other, Merck, is not shown, yet it too has a very liquid options markets. I conduct back tests on these stocks to see if the manic nature of the stock options trading crowd offers any useful information for predicting the future direction of these individual stocks. Similar to the previous Squeeze Play I, Squeeze

Play II aims to identify small pockets of excessive sentiment as an initial trading condition, using a price trigger to get into each trade once that condition is found. Table 9.1 contains Squeeze Play II trading rules, which indicates the use of a slower oscillator.

Instead of an EMA5-21 oscillator, Squeeze Play II uses a EMA50-100 oscillator, which is created by differencing a 50-day exponential moving average with a 100-day exponential moving average (subtracting the 50-day from the 100-day creates the oscillator series).

Squeeze Play II has some additional changes. A long trade is entered when the highest high value of the EMA50-100 in the past 10 days is greater than 5 percent. For short trades, a position is entered when the EMA50-100

Stk	Opt	Name	Call	Put	Total Volume	Days	Total ADV	Call ADV	Put ADV
MSFT	MQF	Microsoft Corporation	355,059	219,264	574,323	21	27,349	16,908	10,441
GE	GE	General Electric Company	218,181	111,822	330,003	21	15,714	10,390	5,325
C	C	Citigroup, Inc.	93,171	183,435	276,606	21	13,172	4,437	8,735
NYB	NQK	New York Community Bancorp	125,338	140,236	265,574	21	12,646	5,968	6,678
TASR	QUR	TASER International, Inc.	157,248	108,195	265,443	21	12,640	7,488	5,152
INTC	INQ	Intel Corporation	146,683	80,051	226,734	21	10,797	6,985	3,812
CYBX	QAJ	Cyberonics, Inc.	136,915	84,258	221,173	21	10,532	6,520	4,012
NT	NT	Nortel Networks Corporation	155,133	45,441	200,574	21	9,551	7,387	2,164
CSCO	CYQ	Cisco Systems, Inc.	140,412	44,946	185,358	21	8,827	6,686	2,140
YHOO	YHQ	Yahoo! Inc.	87,622	75,314	162,936	21	7,759	4,172	3,586
MO	MO	Altria Group, Inc.	71,276	84,560	155,836	21	7,421	3,394	4,027
RJR	RJR	R.J. Reynolds Tobacco Company	65,040	83,565	148,605	21	7,076	3,097	3,979
ORCL	ORQ	Oracle Corporation	110,471	36,683	147,154	21	7,007	5,261	1,747
EP	EPG	El Paso Corporation	95,880	42,610	138,490	21	6,595	4,566	2,029
NOK	NOK	Nokia Corporation ADR	73,549	54,353	127,902	21	6,091	3,502	2,588
TWX	AOL	Time Warner, Inc.	97,100	24,412	121,512	21	5,786	4,624	1,162
RIMM	RUL	Research in Motion Limited	68,603	51,392	119,995	21	5,714	3,267	2,447
EBAY	QXB	eBay, Inc.	51,422	66,519	117,941	21	5,616	2,449	3,168
HPQ	HWP	Hewlett-Packard Company	82,622	34,756	117,378	21	5,589	3,934	1,655
JPM	JPM	J.P. Morgan Chase & Co.	80,819	33,492	114,311	21	5,443	3,849	1,595
WMT	WMT	Wal-Mart Stores, Inc.	66,985	41,485	108,470	21	5,165	3,190	1,975
PFE	PFE	Pfizer Inc.	58,806	45,746	104,552	21	4,979	2,800	2,178
DAL	DAL	Delta Air Lines, Inc.	58,502	42,935	101,437	21	4,830	2,786	2,045
QCOM	QAQ	QUALCOMM, Inc.	59,474	41,152	100,626	21	4,792	2,832	1,960
IMCL	QCI	ImClone Systems Incorporated	65,254	32,282	97,536	21	4,645	3,107	1,537
CPN	CPN	Calpine Corporation	55,722	41,145	96,867	21	4,613	2,653	1,959
TXN	TXN	Texas Instruments Incorporated	53,894	39,330	93,224	21	4,439	2,566	1,873
ALD	CQL	Alllied Capital Corporation	46,084	45,690	91,774	21	4,370	2,194	2,176
GS	GS	The Goldman Sachs Group, Inc.	56,372	34,202	90,574	21	4,313	2,684	1,629
IBM	IBM	International Business Machines Corporation	52,631	36,890	89,521	21	4,263	2,506	1,757
BRCM	RCQ	Broadcom, Inc.	48,797	40,437	89,234	21	4,249	2,324	1,926
AMD	AMD	Advanced Micro Devices, Inc.	46,670	38,113	84,783	21	4,037	2,222	1,815

FIGURE 9.3 CBOE average daily options volume. (*Source:* CBOE.)

TABLE 9.1 EMA50-100 Squeeze Play II Rules

EMA50-100 Squeeze Play II Rules—Entries	
Enter a long position on open when the EMA50-100 highest high value in the past 10 days is *greater* than +5 percent.	Enter a short position on open when the EMA50-100 lowest low value of the past 10 days is *less* than –5 percent.
EMA50-100 Squeeze Play II Rules—Exits	
Exit long positions on open when the EMA50-100 highest high value in the past 10 days is *less* than –5 percent.	Exit short positions on open when the EMA50-100 highest high value in the past 10 days is *greater* than +5 percent.

oscillator's lowest low value of the past 10 days is less than –5 percent. Recall that Squeeze Play I took a trade with an EMA5-21 cross of the zero level. For now, I leave out the price triggers, allowing for a comparative set of test results when using a price trigger later.

SYSTEM LOGIC

When the EMA50-100 has been above zero by 5 percent or more, it means there has been above average *bearishness*, and when it has been below –5 percent there has been above average *bullishness*, which establishes a sufficient sentiment setup. These readings are always taken on a daily closing basis. In other words, if investor psychology is sufficiently one-sided based on these conditions, either too bearish or too bullish, a trade is entered on the next open. I begin with Merck.

Merck, a pharmaceutical giant, has an active options market, and is one of the Dow components. Tests on Merck, as well as the other stocks in this chapter, cover the period of January 7, 1998 through November 26, 2003. I look at long-only trade signals first. Because for now I am only looking for entry points to catch large bullish moves, and this includes a period of major stock declines, any good results from long trades carry extra statistical weight. The results of the non-trigger tests are presented in Table 9.2. As you can see, performance results are calculated in simpler-to-interpret dollar terms; this is not possible for the equity cash indices tested in previous chapters, a limitation found in MetaStock back tests.

TABLE 9.2 EMA50-100 Squeeze Play II with Price Trigger Performance—MRK (Longs Only) 1/7/98–11/26/03

Total net profit	$2,900.45	Average loss	–704.62
		Largest win	$2,347.20
Percent gain/loss	29.00	Largest loss	–$1,668.21
Annual percent gain/loss	4.92	Average length of win	28.26
Initial investment	$10,000.00	Average length of loss	10.89
Buy/Hold profit	–$1,872.39	Longest winning trade	73
Days in test	2,150	Longest losing trade	16
Buy/Hold percentage gain/loss	–18.72	Most consecutive wins	6
Annual B/H percentage gain/loss	–3.18	Most consecutive losses	6
Total closed trades	37	Total bars out	807
		Average length out	21.24
Commissions paid	$375.00		
		Longest out period	154
Average profit per trade	$104.57		
		System close drawdown	–$11.28
Average Win/Average Loss ratio	1.24	Profit/Loss index	18.61
Total long trades	37	System open drawdown	–$211.61
Total winning trades	19	Reward/Risk index	93.20
Total losing trades	18		
		Max open trade drawdown	–$1,650.13
Amount of winning trades	$16,552.18	Buy/Hold index	203.17
Amount of losing trades	–$12,683.08		
Average win	$871.17		

The testing of stocks in MetaStock Professional permits specifying an initial balance. In this book I use $10,000 in all the tests on stocks, which are also margined at 50 percent. Without a price trigger at this stage, Table 9.2 shows results using this $10,000 trading capital that are hardly sufficient for a reasonable system. There are some performance variables that are acceptable, such as a reward/risk ratio of 93.2 and an average win/average loss ratio of 1.24. However, while the buy/hold profit also was exceeded, total net profit was just $2,900.45 for the entire period. Note that buy/hold profit was a negative –$1,872.39, meaning Merck declined during the period studied. Now let's insert a price trigger.

TABLE 9.3 EMA50-100 Squeeze Play II Price Trigger Rules—Entries

Enter long when today's closing price is *greater* than the highest high of the past three days.	Enter short when today's closing price is *less* than the lowest low of the past three days.

TABLE 9.4A EMA50-100 Squeeze Play II Performance with Price Trigger—MRK (Longs Only) 1/7/98–11/26/03. Uses 10 percent maximum loss stop and a trailing stop loss of 50 percent risk with a 9-day price delay

Total net profit	$5,735.56	Average loss	–$590.14
Percent gain/loss	57.36	Largest win	$2,457.41
Annual percent gain/loss	9.74	Largest loss	–$1,552.59
Initial investment	$10,000.00	Average length of win	25.24
		Average length of loss	9.89
Buy/Hold profit	–$1,872.39	Longest winning trade	79
Days in test	2150	Longest losing trade	13
Buy/Hold percent gain/loss	–18.72	Most consecutive wins	6
Annual B/H percent gain/loss	–3.18	Most consecutive losses	3
Total closed trades	26	Total bars out	1007
		Average length out	37.30
Commissions paid	$265.00	Longest out period	168
Average profit per trade	$60.75	System close drawdown	$0.00
		Profit/Loss index	51.92
Average Win/Average Loss ratio	1.21		
Total long trades	26	System open drawdown	–$122.65
Total winning trades	17	Reward/Risk index	97.91
Total losing trades	9		
		Maximum open trade drawdown	–$1,234.55
Amount of winning trades	$12,090.74	Buy/Hold index	350.57
Amount of losing trades	–$5,311.26		
Average win	$711.22		

TABLE 9.4B Optimized EMA50-100 Squeeze Play II Performance with Price Trigger—MRK (Longs Only) 1/7/98–11/26/03. Uses 10 percent maximum loss stop and a trailing stop loss of 50 percent risk with a 9-day price delay

Total net profit	$7,247.34	Average loss	–$344.50
Percent gain/loss	72.47	Largest win	$2,524.08
Annual percent gain/loss	12.30	Largest loss	–$708.26
Initial investment	$10,000.00	Average length of win	28.75
		Average length of loss	11.20
Buy/Hold profit	–$1,872.39	Longest winning trade	79
Days in test	2150	Longest losing trade	12
Buy/Hold percent gain/loss	–18.72	Most consecutive wins	5
Annual Buy/Hold percent gain/loss	–3.18	Most consecutive losses	3
Total closed trades	17	Total bars out	1106
		Average length out	61.44
Commissions paid	$175.00	Longest out period	235
Average profit per trade	$493.59	System close drawdown	$0.00
Average Win/Average Loss ratio	2.45	Profit/Loss index	80.
Winning long trades	12	System open drawdown	–$122.65
Total winning trades	12	Reward/Risk index	98.34
Total losing trades	5	Maximum open trade drawdown	–$1,143.74
Amount of winning trades	$10,113.58	Buy/Hold index	425.98
Amount of losing trades	–$1,722.49		
Average win	$842.80		

Again testing longs only, Table 9.3 contains the addition of a price trigger with Squeeze Play II. The system enters a long position on open given the sentiment conditions described in Table 9.1, and when the closing price of the day is greater than the highest high of the past three days (the price trigger). For short positions, when the closing price of the day is less than the lowest low of the past three days, a short position is entered on the next open. Table 9.3 contains these new price trigger rules.

Results from testing Squeeze Play II with the price trigger rules described in Table 9.3 are presented in Table 9.4A. A stop loss of 10 percent and trail-

TABLE 9.5 EMA50-100 Squeeze Play II Performance with Optimized Price Trigger—MRK (Longs Only) 1/7/98–11/26/03 (Note: Same stop loss management specified in Tables 9.4A and 9.4B was used in these tests.)

Optimization of Highest High Days Trigger

Profit %	Net Profit($)	Total Trades	Winners	Losers	Ratio Winners to Losers Days	Days Optimization Variable
75.46	7,545.8750	18	13	5	1.7012	3
59.57	5,957.1211	22	14	8	1.2434	2
53.40	5,340.2178	16	10	6	2.1766	5
47.66	4,766.0752	23	15	8	1.0791	1
45.38	4,537.8652	18	11	7	1.6968	4

ing stop of 50 percent with a 9-day price delay are also added. Total net profit increases from $2,900.45 to $5,735.56, with a very good buy/hold index rating of 350.57. Anything greater than 100 shows the buy/hold amount was exceeded. The annual gain is 9.74 percent, which beats an annual buy/hold loss of –3.18 percent. The system had a risk/reward index of 97.91 (100 is the best) and a very small open system drawdown of –$122.65. All these are excellent results, especially since this is for long trades only during a period when Merck suffered declines.

To further test the validity of these results I now run some optimization routines on trigger thresholds in the model. The results are presented in Table 9.5. The best profit was obtained by using a close above the highest high day over the previous three days for the price trigger, but all produced a profit—of good indication for this system.

SYSTEM TESTING ON SHORT TRADES

Now I want to work the short side into the model, given that we have fairly good results from the long side for a stock that suffered some large declines during the study period. The setup uses +5/–5 percent thresholds as specified in Table 9.1 for short/long entry and exit points and 3-day high/low-close price triggers breakout points (leaving the same stops in place used above). Table 9.6 shows the results on Merck using parameters for short position trades only, with results that easily beat the buy/hold annualized

TABLE 9.6 EMA50-100 Squeeze Play II Performance with Price Trigger—MRK (Shorts Only) 1/7/98–11/26/03

Total net profit	$6,202.56	Average loss	–$572.93
Percent gain/loss	62.03	Largest win	$2,389.54
Annual percent gain/loss	10.53	Largest loss	–$1,378.16
Initial investment	$10,000.00	Average length of win	16.33
		Average length of loss	8.75
Buy/Hold profit	–1872.39	Longest winning trade	51
Days in test	2150	Longest losing trade	12
Buy/Hold percent gain/loss	–18.72	Most consecutive wins	5
Annual Buy/Hold percent gain/loss	–3.18		
Total closed trades	26	Total bars out	1170
		Average length out	43.33
Commissions paid	$260.00		
		Longest out period	257
Average profit per trade	$238.56		
		System close drawdown	–$966.15
Average Win/Average Loss ratio	1.05	Profit/Loss index	57.51
Total short trades	26	System open drawdown	–$970.55
Winning short trades	18	Reward/Risk index	86.47
Total losing trades	8		
		Maximum open trade drawdown	–$1,257.18
Amount of winning trades	$10,785.99	Buy/Hold index	431.26
Amount of losing trades	–$4,583.43		
Average win	$599.22		

loss of –3.18 percent. Total net profit is $6,202.56 with an annualized gain of 10.53 percent with acceptable performance variables.

When an optimization test run is applied to a range of sentiment thresholds, performance improves slightly. However, more interesting is the appearance of the same wide band of profitable entry/exit threshold parameter values. Recall that I began this study with a best guess of +5/–5 percent thresholds for entry/exit. In both long and short optimization runs, all combinations of nearby sentiment thresholds produced good to excellent profits. The results for long trades are presented in Table 9.7, which uses the original

TABLE 9.7 Oscillator Optimized EMA50-100 Squeeze Play II Performance with Price Trigger—MRK (Longs only). 1/7/98–11/26/03. Uses 10 percent maximum loss stop and a trailing stop loss of 50 percent risk with a 9-day price delay.

Net Profit	Percent Gain	Total Trades	Winning	Losing Average	Win/ Average Loss	Short exit threshold optimization parameters	Short entry threshold optimization parameters
$23,447.21	234.47	39	31	8	1.5023	8	–7
$21,664.41	216.64	41	31	10	1.469	8	–6
$21,339.72	213.40	42	31	11	1.3695	8	–5
$20,707.59	207.08	48	34	14	1.3558	5	–7
$19,599.17	195.99	49	35	14	1.1944	5	–6
$18,796.62	187.97	35	27	8	1.4484	8	–8
$18,124.88	181.25	53	35	18	1.2592	5	–5
$16,938.73	169.39	44	33	11	1.0621	6	–7
$16,560.07	165.60	45	34	11	0.9427	6	–6
$16,382.46	163.82	49	34	15	1.1321	6	–5
$16,209.81	162.10	43	31	12	1.2181	8	–4
$15,994.69	159.95	51	34	17	1.2704	4	–7
$15,351.55	153.52	58	39	19	1.2373	2	–6
$15,310.91	153.11	44	32	12	1.1363	8	–3
$15,156.94	151.57	57	38	19	1.2538	2	–7
$14,970.21	149.70	52	35	17	1.147	4	–6
$14,612.93	146.13	61	38	23	1.3783	2	–5
$14,001.01	140.01	54	36	18	1.0734	5	–4

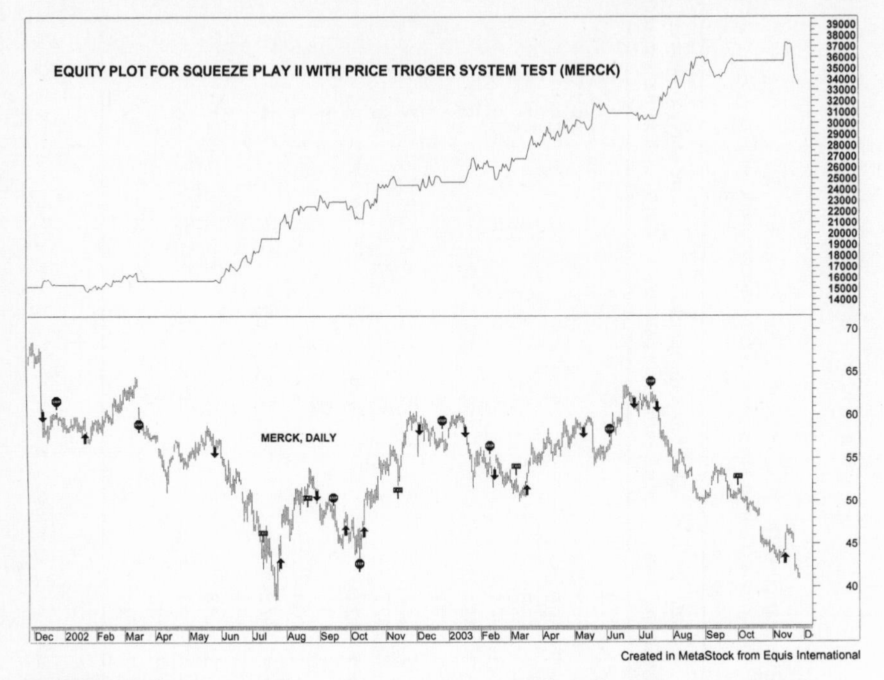

FIGURE 9.4 Squeeze Play II System test on Merck, indicating entry and exit points, and equity plot.

price trigger from Table 9.3; a maximum stop loss of 10 percent along with a trailing stop of 50 percent with a 9-day delay, this is also used for all the other tests on stocks below. The account, moreover, is still trading on 50 percent margin.

Note the columns of the sentiment threshold variable in Table 9.7. There is a very good profitable profile for every combination. For example, the +8/–8 percent threshold levels produced a gain of 187.97 percent during this six-year period, or a total of $18,796.62 on an original investment of $10,000. A look at the other combinations indicates the system holds together quite well across a wide band of excessive sentiment levels.

Finally, let's put this all together and apply the system to a long and short trades simultaneous test, which can produce trading synergies as reverse signals act to limit losses, and possibly produce additional gains.

Table 9.8 contains the results of a long/short test on Merck with thresholds optimized. The maximum net profit was $82,602.55 with a reward/risk index of 99.71 with no closed system drawdown or open system drawdown, and annual gain of 140.23 percent. It does not get much better than this,

TABLE 9.8 Optimized EMA50-100 Squeeze Play II Performance with Price Trigger—MRK (Longs/Shorts) Uses 10 percent maximum stop loss of 50 percent risk with a 9-day price delay and 50 percent margin. (1/7/98–11/26/03)

Total net profit	$82,602.55	Average win	$3,941.61
		Average loss	–$2,827.67
Percent gain/loss	826.03	Largest win	$26,473.34
Annual percent gain/loss	140.23		
Initial investment	$10,000.00	Largest loss	–$10,289.17
		Average length of win	21.61
Buy/Hold profit	–$3,739.78	Average length of loss	6.86
Days in test	2150	Longest winning trade	79
Buy/Hold percent gain/loss	–37.4	Longest losing trade	12
Annual Buy/Hold percent gain/loss	–6.35	Most consecutive wins	6
Total closed trades	45	Most consecutive losses	2
		Total bars out	805
Commissions paid	$450.00	Average length out	17.89
Average profit per trade	$1,835.61	Longest out period	113
Average Win/ Average Loss ratio	1.39	System close drawdown	$0.00
Total long trades	18	Profit/Loss index	67.60
Total short trades	27	System open drawdown	–240.29
Winning long trades	13	Reward/Risk index	99.71
Winning short trades	18	Maximum open trade drawdown	–$7,631.17
Total winning trades	31	Buy/Hold index	2308.75
Total losing trades	14		
Amount of winning trades	$122,189.95		
Amount of losing trades	–$39,587.41		

especially with an average-win-to-average-loss ratio of 1.39. Figure 9.4 shows the trigger point entries generated by the system back test, catching some very large moves made by Merck. But just how reliable are these results, since they are optimized? The answer requires an examination of the results of the optimization routine on all combinations of the threshold values, which are presented in Table 9.9; and it requires further testing on other stocks with these same system parameters.

TABLE 9.9 Optimized EMA50-100 Squeeze Play II Performance with Price Trigger—MRK (Longs/Shorts) Uses 10 percent maximum loss stop and a trailing stop loss of 50 percent risk with a 9-day price delay and 50 percent margin

Net Profit	Percent Gain	Total Trades	Winning	Losing Average	Win/ Average Loss	Long entry/short exit sentiment threshold optimization parameters	Short entry/long exit sentiment threshold optimization parameters
$82,602.5547	826.03	45	31	14	1.3939	8	–5
$81,426.2656	814.26	42	31	11	1.2583	8	–7
$80,160.6094	801.61	44	31	13	1.3944	8	–6
$79,826.4141	798.26	52	35	17	1.2889	5	–6
$77,486.7656	774.87	51	34	17	1.3366	5	–7
$72,821.9609	728.22	46	31	15	1.4017	8	–4
$70,182.2578	701.82	56	35	21	1.3643	5	–5
$61,416.5391	614.17	57	36	21	1.25	5	–4
$55,446.6836	554.47	51	34	17	1.2041	7	–5
$52,217.1094	522.17	49	32	17	1.217	8	–3
$50,441.9492	504.42	36	25	11	1.1444	8	–8
$49,210.6016	492.11	47	33	14	1.1032	7	–7
$48,389.6914	483.9	49	33	16	1.1806	7	–6
$47,319.832	473.2	52	34	18	1.1878	7	–4
$45,073.1016	450.73	51	33	18	1.2565	6	–6
$45,027.2852	450.27	52	32	20	1.4451	8	–2
$44,870.3008	448.7	56	35	21	1.2434	4	–6
$44,146.5234	441.47	71	44	27	1.1299	2	–3
$43,755.3906	437.55	55	34	21	1.2746	4	–7
$41,873.7461	418.74	55	33	22	1.394	6	–5
$41,537.4922	415.37	60	37	23	1.0931	5	–3
$41,498.2031	414.98	50	32	18	1.2811	6	–7
$41,320.2734	413.2	60	35	25	1.345	4	–5
$40,139.168	401.39	45	28	17	1.1895	5	–8
$36,191.9805	361.92	56	34	22	1.2706	6	–4
$35,698.7266	356.99	61	36	25	1.2347	4	–4

The worst combination of the threshold +4/–4 percent produced a net profit of $35,698.72 and a total gain of 356.99 percent (last entry in Table 9.9), which indicates that these parameters all work quite well, at least on Merck. In other words, any of the sentiment thresholds used would have generated fairly good results. Will I get the same favorable results on other stocks? The next step in testing requires running this system on the other equity issues I've selected, which should give us some clues.

OUT-OF-SAMPLE TESTING ON OTHER LARGE-CAP STOCKS

If the system developed in this chapter has a chance of success, it must be able to perform well on more than just one stock. In other words, the system performance must be robust, and one way to explore this dimension is through an out-of-sample test on other stocks. Typically this is performed on the same stock or market using a time period different from that used to derive the performance parameters. Out-of-sample tests are important because the past may not repeat itself exactly in the future. Ideally, an out-of-sample test should yield similar performance to the initial sample tests, without altering key threshold parameters. More important, however, is to see if the same results, without any further optimization, can be obtained from other stocks.

As already mentioned, similarities exist between the stocks selected for this study despite being from different industry groups. The common characteristics are that they are large-cap stocks with actively traded options markets. This is an important preselection criterion. The market for options must be very liquid in order to effectively capture the option trading crowd's sentiment. Recall that the theory of crowd behavior in options markets rests on the premise that the unsophisticated or amateurish options trader, while perhaps a rational individual in isolation, behaves emotionally as part of a group, making predictable misjudgments at market extremes. The higher the degree of public involvement, represented by greater liquidity, the more likely the theory will work. The greater the overall volume of options trade, in other words, the better the results should be: This is statistically more significant in terms of representing the sentiment of the options trading crowd.

With this in mind, I present the results from running Squeeze Play II on a group of stocks with liquid options markets in Table 9.10. The tests are

TABLE 9.10 Summary of Results for Squeeze Play II Run on IBM, Citigroup, Merck, Wal-Mart, General Electric, and Microsoft (Optimized)

Stock	Net Profit	Percent Gain/Loss	Total Trades	Winning	Losing
IBM	$4,754.38	47.54	41	18	23
C	$44,793.34	417.93	17	12	5
MRK	$82,602.55	826.03	45	31	14
WMT	–$4,675.28	–46.75	34	16	18
GE	$14,228.01	142.20	78	39	39
MSFT	$15,454.00	154.54	46	23	23
Total	$157,157.00	1,571.49	261	139	122

conducted on IBM, Citigroup, Merck, Wal-Mart, General Electric, and Microsoft (MSFT). During the period of the study, the aggregate equity grew from $60,000 to $217,157, a total net profit of $157,157, as seen in Table 9.10. The testing actually covers just five and a half years (not six) because the moving averages need 100 days before they can begin to be calculated. The annualized rate of return, therefore, actually comes to 47.6 percent. While this performance appears adequate, further study is necessary to determine why certain stocks perform better than others. Ideally, this approach should be applied across a much larger basket of stocks to diversify risk (as is common with standard portfolio risk management) with the employment of multiple sentiment threshold parameters to diversify entry/exit entry points.

Finally, with *no optimization* of the threshold variables, and using the original +5/–5 percent values, I ran the test again on all the stocks: the results, which were impressive, did not beat the buy/hold level of profit, as

TABLE 9.11 Summary of Results for Squeeze Play II Run on IBM, Citigroup, Merck, Wal-Mart, General Electric, and Microsoft (Nonoptimized)

Stock	Net Profit	Buy/Hold Profit	Percent Gain/Loss
IBM	$564.13	$14,205.71	5.64
C	$14,258.93	$15,309.93	142.59
MRK	$70,182.26	–$3,736.65	701.82
WMT	–$8,334.31	$36,372.33	–83.34
GE	–$1,565.92	$3,425.43	–15.66
MSFT	–$3,339.19	$29,297.40	–33.39
Total	$71,786.21	$94,874.15	717.66

presented in Table 9.11. The total net profit for the group was $71,786.21 compared with a total buy/hold profit of $94,874.15. Total percent gain was 717.66 for the group of stocks, but was heavily dependent on the performances of Merck, since the remainders were largely a wash. I would like to see earnings more evenly spread across all the stocks. To fully evaluate Squeeze Play II on stocks, moreover, it would require a much larger sample than six issues, which is outside the scope of this book. Properly done, though, this system clearly has huge potential if applied to a larger portfolio of stocks.

SUMMARY

Based on tests in this chapter using put/call ratios for individual stocks, there is clearly an inefficiency in these markets that allows astute traders to capitalize on the ebb and flow of excessive fear and greed. Here, too, it pays to watch the equity option buyers and trade against this crowd. However, testing Squeeze Play II, it was shown that performance underperformed the buy/hold approach as a group. In the next chapter, I continue to look for pockets of market inefficiency again using put/call ratios on stocks to see if it is possible to develop an even better system. One such system uses Squeeze Play II combined with long-term equity options (LEAPS) to avoid the detrimental effect of stop losses, and to maximize leverage.

CHAPTER 10

Squeeze Play II and LEAPS Surrogates

Given the mixed system test results using Squeeze Play II in the previous chapter, I now attempt to apply a variation of Squeeze Play II to the same group of stocks using LEAPS, long-term equity options. LEAPS serve as surrogates to buying or shorting the underlying stock. Again, the premise is that the option trading crowd sentiment, at extremes, is tradable information despite what theorists of efficient markets and random walk disciples claim.

In the modified Squeeze Play II applied in this chapter, I keep the same entry rules but adjust the exit plan, which includes the removal of all stops. Recall that the original setup used a 10 percent maximum stop loss and a trailing stop that risks 50 percent of any unrealized profit in a trade (with a 9-day delay price). The exit plan now uses a time stop. In this approach, that is, the exit is set at three different fixed time intervals, which is why I refer to them as time stops. This exit approach is deployed in future chapters as well. The exits occur at T + 30 (30 days into the trade), T + 60, and T + 90 days into the trades; in effect, there are three trading systems, since each has a different exit rule. By creating a triple exit strategy, I hope to be able to apply some of the knowledge gained during the statistical tests performed in Chapters 4, 5, and 6, which examined performance of put/call ratios across long- and short-term time frames. The trading rules are presented in Table 10.1, and Figures 10.1 and 10.2 illustrate the oscillator and a long trade.

The first phase of tests is based on using stocks, not options, for trading. Then I replace the use of stocks for trading with LEAPS as surrogates. The LEAPS used are in the money, which allows for defined risk before entering the trade but unlimited profit potential. Furthermore, with no (or very little) time value, there is no (or very little) time value decay; addi-

TABLE 10.1 Modified EMA50-100 Squeeze Play II Rules: All Stop Losses Were Removed

Modified EMA50-100 Squeeze Play II Rules—Entries	
Enter a long position on open when EMA50-100 highest high value in the past 10 days is greater than +5 percent.	Enter a short position on open when the EMA50-100 lowest low value of the past 10 days is less than −5 percent.

Modified of EMA50-100 Squeeze Play II Rules—Exits	
Exit long positions at T + 30-, T + 60-, and T + 90-day lagged periods from entry of trade.	Exit short positions at T + 30-, T + 60-, and T + 90-day lagged periods from entry of trade.

tionally, there are not many associated issues of volatility with which to contend. To learn more about LEAPS, the Chicago Board Options Exchange offers wonderful educational tools for those interested in these very useful trading vehicles. My Web site, TradingAgainstTheCrowd.com, also offers a primer on LEAPS.

Table 10.2 contains the results of the system tests performed on the same group of stocks used in the previous chapter. The total buy/hold profit for each stock is included, as well. Each stock trades $10,000 on each time frame, as these are actually considered separate trading systems. For example, IBM has one system running with a T + 30 exit and another with T + 60, each with initial investments of $10,000. The buy/hold totals are seen in Table 10.2 in the last column on the right. Taken as a group, the buy/hold approach is not exceeded by the total profit generated by the systems running on six stocks ($290,377.41 versus $135,033.40). The initial investment to trade the systems is $180,000.

If we take just the T + 30 time frame for shorts (recall from Chapters 4, 5, and 6 that the best results and the only time frame worth trading are the shortest ones) and all the long-trade time frames, total profit for these systems increases to $167,075.22. This amount is higher than that of the group as a whole, but still does not beat the buy/hold approach for the group. Performance of this variation of Squeeze Play II, therefore unfortunately underperforms, even though it is profitable.

Instead of using traditional stops for risk management, a better approach is to trade with LEAPS. This permits trades to catch some of these big moves without getting whipped (stopped) out of a position by too early an

TABLE 10.2 Modified Squeeze Play II Test Results Summary—No Stops Using T + 30 through T + 90 Time Frames as Exits

	T + 30 Longs	T + 60 Longs	T + 90 Longs	T + 30 Shorts
IBM	$16,373.73	–$ 337.67	$ 6,294.62	$18,618.19
C	$11,715.04	–$ 6,429.00	–$ 1,394.29	–$ 80,76.92
MRK	–$ 4,941.92	–$ 3,327.43	–$ 3,458.26	$28,001.95
WMT	$13,253.49	$21,092.37	$32,174.91	–$ 6,555.94
GE	–$ 7,101.84	–$ 8,718.74	–$ 3,624.59	–$ 4,935.58
MSFT	$18,170.95	$26,611.64	$43,300.11	–$ 9,630.13
Total	$47,469.45	$28,891.17	$73,292.50	$17,421.57

	T + 60 Shorts	T + 90 Shorts	Total Profit	Buy/Hold Profit
IBM	$ 6,813.48	–$3,190.12	$ 44,572.23	$ 38,150.67
C	–$ 5,950.40	–$9,371.81	–$ 19,507.40	$ 35,108.10
MRK	$15,028.82	–$ 440.13	$ 30,863.03	$ 5,028.65
WMT	–$ 9,077.83	–$9,139.32	$ 41,747.68	$115,429.15
GE	$ 810.24	–$4,099.29	–$ 27,669.8	$ 11,213.29
MSFT	–$ 6,015.50	–$7,409.44	$ 65,027.63	$ 85,447.55
Total	$ 1,608.81	–$3,650.19	$135,033.40	$290,377.41

TABLE 10.3 Modified Squeeze Play II Test Results Summary—LEAPS Using T + 30 through T + 90 Time Frames as Exits

	T + 30 Longs	T + 60 Longs	T + 90 Longs	T + 30 Shorts
IBM	$ 37,135.83	$ 19,869.53	$ 48,302.92	$29,322.19
C	$ 20,702.51	$ 795.86	$ 2,035.06	–$ 3,077.04
MRK	$ 2,327.06	$ 5,630.18	$ 6,350.77	$32,836.79
WMT	$ 26,232.69	$ 29,283.00	$ 39,843.60	–$ 1,374.42S
GE	–$ 3,616.97	$ 1,052.41	$ 7,690.51	$ 5,145.82
MSFT	$ 65,653.25	$ 47,152.64	$ 80,943.01	–$ 3,988.93
Total	$148,434.40	$103,783.60	$185,165.90	$60,238.83

	T + 60 Shorts	T + 90 Shorts	Total Profit	Buy/Hold Profit
IBM	$ 9,933.41	$ 4,140.41	$148,704.30	$ 38,150.67
C	$ 4,140.90	$ 2,422.69	$ 27,019.98	$ 35,108.10
MRK	$20,516.44	$12,228.17	$ 79,889.41	$ 5,025.65
WMT	–$ 3,117.79	–$ 2,268.77	$ 89,972.73	$115,429.15
GE	$15,874.54	$ 1,822.13	$ 27,968.44	$ 11,273.29
MSFT	$ 812.29	–$ 2,869.02	$187,703.20	$ 85,447.55
Total	$48,159.79	$15,475.61	$560,754.83	$290,377.41

entry or by other market noise before the move actually occurs. Table 10.3 contains the results of Squeeze Play II using LEAPS, which does not need stops for risk management because maximum loss is known prior to entering each trade.

Total profit for the entire group of stocks and time frames now increases to $560,754.83, well above the buy/hold total of $290,377.41. This represents a 51% annualized return versus a buy/hold return of 27%.

If the T + 30 short position trades and T + 30 through T + 90 long position trades are the only ones taken, total net profit for these systems comes to $497,622.73. This can be compared favorably with buy/hold profits of $290,377.41. But while improvement over the non-LEAPS approach for these time frames is achieved, it does not do better than the group as a whole.

Last, we might want to eliminate all short position trades when using this LEAPS approach. We can aim instead to try to catch only the long bull moves following bearish sentiment extremes. In this case, the T + 30,

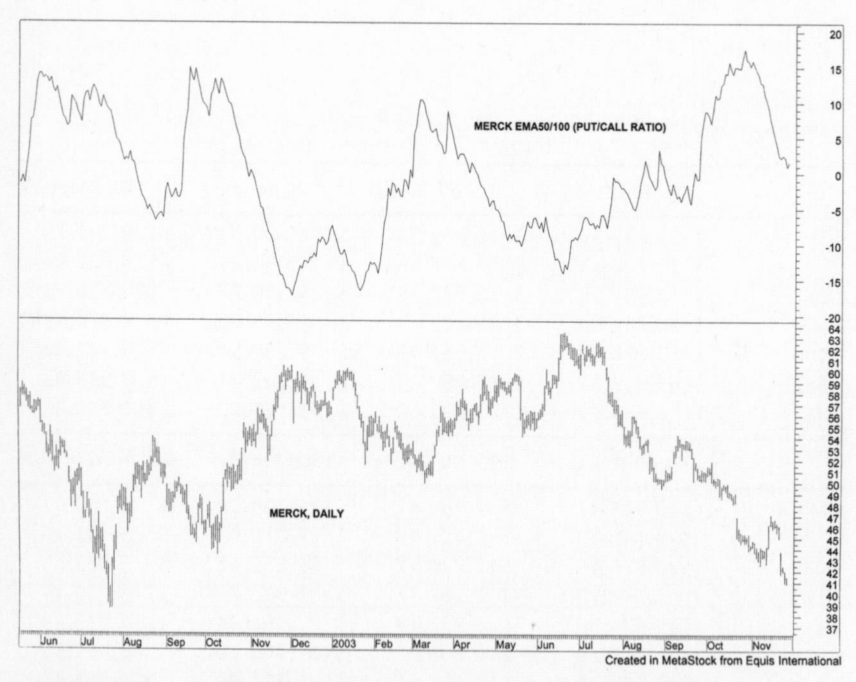

FIGURE 10.1 EMA50-100 for Merck put/call ratio with Merck daily prices.

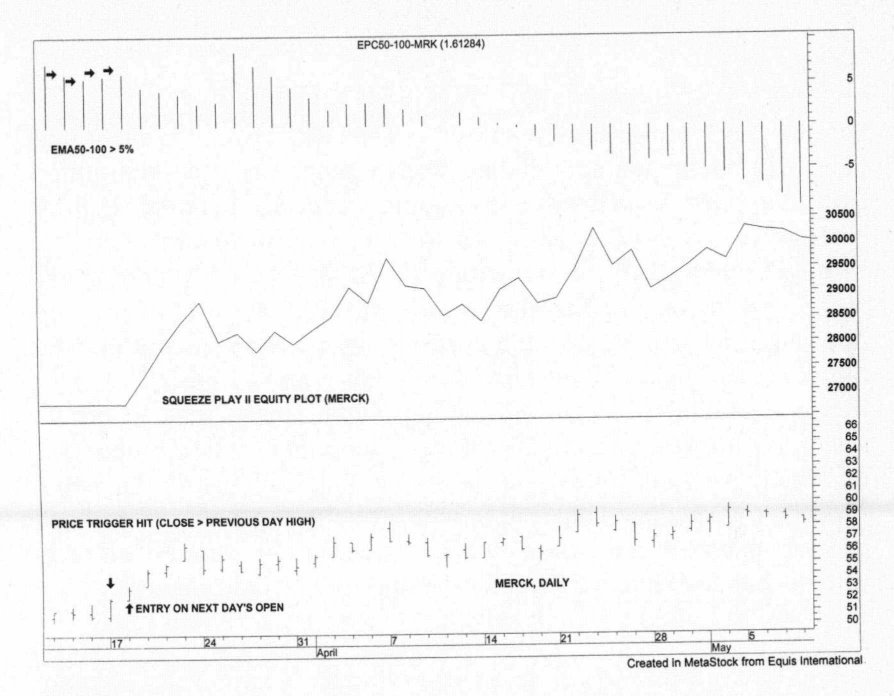

FIGURE 10.2 EMA50-100 for Merck put/call ratios with Merck daily prices. Long entry and exit arrows for system.

T + 60, and T + 90 long position trades only (just call option trades) produces a profit of $437,383.90 versus a buy/hold profit of $290,377.41, beating the important benchmark by over $147,006.49!

The initial capital investment for these three long position only systems is $30,000 for each stock in the group, still a total of $180,000. This results, therefore, in a total gain of 243 percent, or annualized rate of return over six years of 40 percent for the total group—not too shabby for taking just long trades. While you might make the case that this is cherry picking the best periods, previous tests substantiated that it is very difficult to make money on short trades using put/call ratios thus providing support for such an approach. Therefore, taking long position trades aimed at catching big bearish sentiment wave reversals would make perfect sense. The options trading crowd is usually the most incorrect at market bottoms, moves that appear to be captured quite well using Squeeze Play II with in-the-money LEAPs call options as surrogates to trading with the underlying stock.

SUMMARY

Squeeze Play II proves itself once again when using a variation on the exit plan. With maximum and trailing stops removed and predetermined exit "time stops" used instead, the system produced good total net profits. However, it was not large enough to beat the buy/hold level of profits. However, when LEAPS are substituted for stocks, total net profit jumps well above the buy/hold level with an annualized return of 51 percent. Applying what was learned in a previous statistical analysis of put/call ratio on stock indices, trading only in the shortest time frame (T + 30) for shorts, and taking all long time frames on all the stocks, total net profits easily surpasses total buy/hold profits but does not beat total group profits. Finally, the results were good when the short trades were eliminated altogether, taking just long trades, with a total percentage profit of 243 percent, an annualized gain of 40 percent. This also compares favorably with the buy/hold rate of return for the same period of 27 percent.

CHAPTER 11

The Tsunami Sentiment Wave Trading System

I am never satisfied with just one approach; I know that it is smart to combine trading systems and diversify the markets to which the systems are applied. I therefore explore another dimension in this chapter that is a further variation of the idea of trading against the options crowd used in previous chapters. Again, I use the same group of stocks for testing and to provide a basis for comparison.

Since there is considerable noise in these individual stock options markets, I now attempt to reduce the number of trades by identifying the most extreme zones and entering trades only at these levels, for predetermined long-term holds that vary in length.

I call this approach the Tsunami Sentiment Wave (TSW) System because it aims to catch the biggest sentiment waves for long rides instead of all the smaller ripples of inefficiency measured in less extreme bullish and bearish sentiment zones.

This approach is best done with in-the-money LEAPS on stocks because just like with Squeeze Play I no stops are required, and it effectively acts as a surrogate to purchasing or shorting the underlying stock, thus allowing for greater leverage of capital. The leverage increases to 90 percent because $10,000 of starting capital (the model account used in this book) allows trades with LEAPS up to an equivalent stock position of $90,000. For example, if the stock is trading at $100 per share and $10,000 is applied, the stock position size would be 100 shares. (This is the equivalent of one LEAPS option, since options are denominated in 100-share units). But the LEAPS option would require only about $1,000 to $1,500 in capital.

Since in-the-money LEAPS allow for creating surrogate stock positions with only 10–15 percent of the capital needed for these stock positions, there is much more leverage available. Assuming again a stock trading at $100, therefore, you could buy a LEAPS option for about $1,500 and get the same profit potential (minus any small time premium in the option, if any) that a $10,000 stock position offers. Maximum risk on the position, meanwhile, would be just $1,500 (about 15 percent of starting equity). Since we know maximum loss going into the trade, there is no need to use traditional stops. This can dramatically change performance, because the underlying stock has lots of wiggle room, without the risk of getting stopped out of a trade. Each trade, therefore, risks up to 15 percent of equity.

TSUNAMI SENTIMENT WAVE SETUP

TSW system rules are quite simple and are presented in Table 11.1. As with the Squeeze Play II, there are three exit time frames used for longs and shorts: T + 30, T + 60, and T + 90 days. But the wave speed has been slowed down to EMA21-50 from EMA50-100 used in Squeeze Play II. The system works as a long and short system, but no *reversals* from short-to-long or long-to-short occur if already in a trade. In other words, if a short signal is generated while in a long position, the trade is ignored. The same holds true for long signals when in a short position. When a trade is entered, a LEAPS option is purchased and held until the time stop is reached (i.e., T + 30, T + 60, T + 90). This means that if a short signal is generated while in a LEAPS call position, the LEAPS long call position is still held open and no LEAPS put position is established until the time stop of T + 30, 60, or 90 days is reached. The same applies to open LEAPS put option positions.

As you can see in Table 11.2, total net profit from the TSW system using LEAPS was greater than the buy/hold total by $196,067, with a total

TABLE 11.1 Tsunami Sentiment Wave Trading Rules

Long Entry	Short Entry
Enter a long position on open when EMA21-50 is *greater* than 10 percent and there are no open short positions.	Enter a short position on open when EMA21-50 is *less* than −10 percent and there are no open long positions.
Long Exit	**Short Exit**
Exit a long position on open in three steps: at T + 30, T + 60, T + 90 days.	Exit a short position on open in three steps: at T + 30, T + 60, T + 90 days.

TABLE 11.2 Performance of TSW System Based on $10,000 in Trading Capital Applied to Each Stock for Each Time Frame, or a Total of $180,000 for All Subsystems

	Non-LEAPS Performance			LEAPS Performance		
	T + 30	**T + 60**	**T + 90**	**T + 30**	**T + 60**	**T + 90**
GE	8,133	18,240	31,973	22,767	26,568	36,774
MSFT	−1,971	−5,381	6,607	8,326	11,744	13,132
IBM	4,126	13,745	28,674	16,192	24,935	32,597
WMT	42,087	12,472	−7,644	49,560	19,438	−262.71
C	−9,940	−7,015	−6,338	−2,678	512.67	4,173
MRK	28,737	130,480	12,745	47,691	157,634	25,561
TSW Profit	71,172	162,541	73,661	141,858	240,832	111,974
Buy/Hold Profit	108,372	106,054	84,171	108,372	106,054	84,171
TSW-Buy/Hold Profit	−37,200	56,487	−10,510	33,486	134,777	27,803

buy/hold profit of $298,597 and total LEAPS net profit of $494,664. Compare this to a non-LEAPS approach, which generated a $307,374 profit against a buy/hold return of $298,597. Total percent gain was 275 percent, with an annualized rate of return of 50 percent. The tests cover a period of 5.5 years, as in the previous chapter.

Figure 11.1 shows Tsunami Sentiment Wave threshold extremes (+10% and −10%) for GE, which indicated key turning points. A look a Figure 11.2 reveals how these extreme thresholds can correctly indentify key turning points, as the long entry point for Merck shows.

The buy-and-hold profit rate for the group was 16 percent on an annualized basis. Looking at individual time frames for LEAP performance, T + 60 produced the best returns with a gain of $240,832, a total return of 401 percent, or an annualized gain of 72.9 percent, compared with a buy/hold annual rate of return of 32 percent for this time frame. The worst time frame using the TSW LEAPS strategy was T + 90, with $111,974 in total net profit, or an annual rate of return of 34 percent, but above the buy/hold level of $84,171 for this time frame. As for the best period in terms of profit differential over buy/hold profits, the T + 60 was superior, with $240,832 versus $106,054 for the buy/hold approach. T + 30, meanwhile, produced $141,858 in total net profit.

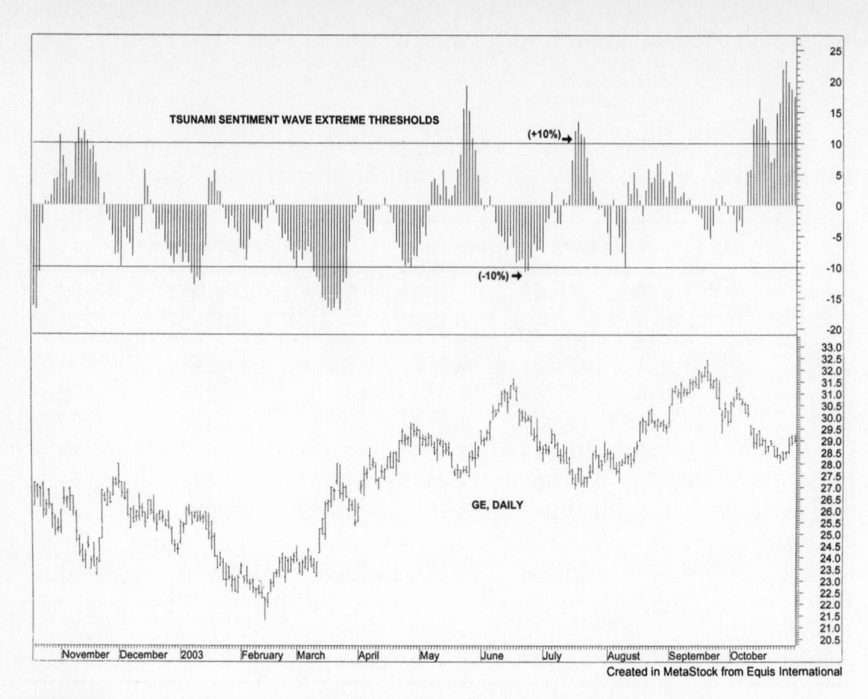

FIGURE 11.1 Tsunami sentiment wave chart with EMA21-50 and GE.

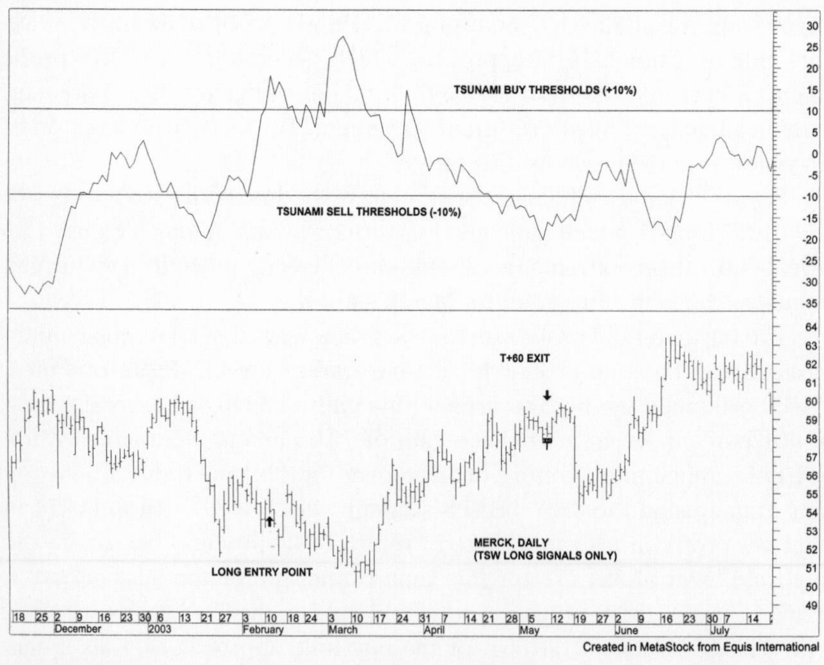

FIGURE 11.2 TSW system test showing entry and exit arrows for MRK test found in Table 11.3.

While TSW with LEAPS is not quite as good as Squeeze Play II, it still has excellent returns overall, especially in the T + 30 and T + 60 time frames. Table 11.3 shows results from testing on the top-performing stock in this series of tests. Merck in the T + 60 period had total net profits without LEAPS of $130,480 and total net profits with LEAPS of $157,634.

The test results on Merck presented in Table 11.3 show how this system has the ability to produce stellar profits on the right stocks. With no closed system drawdown and a reward/risk index of 97.87, trading does not get better than this—especially without any consecutive losses and 15 winning

TABLE 11.3 Tsunami Sentiment Wave Trading Merck (T + 60) (LEAPS profit = +$157,633.62)

Total net profit	$130,480.52	Average win	$13,569.68
Percent gain/loss	1,304.81	Average loss	–$14,612.93
		Largest win	$40,965.02
Annual percent gain/loss	225.29	Largest loss	–$59,223.92
Initial investment	$10,000	Average length of win	62.00
		Average length of loss	62.00
		Longest winning trade	62
Buy/Hold profit	–1091.41	Longest losing trade	62
		Most consecutive wins	5
Days in test	2,114	Most consecutive losses	1
Buy/Hold percent gain/loss	–10.91	Total bars out	1,437
Annual Buy/Hold percent gain/loss	–1.88	Average length out	68.43
		Longest out period	113
Total closed trades	20	System close drawdown	$0.00
Commissions paid	0.00	Profit/Loss index	64.10
Average profit per trade	$6,524.03	System open drawdown	–$2,838.85
Average Win/Average Loss ratio	0.93	Reward/Risk index	97.87
Total long trades	11	Max open trade drawdown	–$59,223.92
Total short trades	9	Buy/Hold index	12,055.25
Winning long trades	7		
Winning short trades	8		
Total winning trades	15		
Total losing trades	5		
Amount of winning trades	$203,545.16		
Amount of losing trades	–$73,064.63		

trades out of a total of 20. The maximum open trade drawdown and open system drawdown, while high, is not of any concern since the LEAPS have limited losses by definition. Thus, we can ignore these numbers as they do not reflect actual trading using options, since we know losses are limited to a maximum of 15 percent of equity.

SUMMARY

Trading at only the most extreme levels of the EMA21-50—defined by a deviation from the average sentiment of this wave by 10 percent (extreme bearishness = long entries) and –10 percent (extreme bullishness = short entries) and removing all triggers and stops—the Tsunami Sentiment Wave (TSW) system only slightly beat the buy-and-hold net profit for the three time frames used as subsystems. Yet, when LEAPS are substituted for owning or shorting the stock itself, the system shows great promise, with an annualized rate of return for the three time frames of 50 percent. Buy-and-hold annualized return for the period, assuming fully invested positions margined at 50 percent (the same assumption throughout this book for all stocks), was 32 percent. Using the equity-only put/call contract volume ratio for each of the stocks in the study, therefore, it appears that, on average, traders of individual stock options also make excellent contrarian sentiment indicators.

CHAPTER 12

Adapting Put/Call Ratios to Bond Futures

Similar to the stock market, the options trading crowd can be relied upon to furnish the fuel needed to power bond market trades to profitability. The same dynamic of crowd psychology, identified with bond option put/call ratios, can be found to work in the market for bond futures.

If you are not familiar with futures markets, a futures contract is merely a derivative instrument. This is a fancy way of saying that it get its value from underlying real assets, in this case 30-year U.S. Treasury bonds. My previous book *Options on Futures, New Trading Strategies* provides an excellent introduction to futures and futures options, including some classic trading strategies. Of course, there are many other books, and I encourage you to consult as many as possible before getting started trading futures. For now, you only need to know the following product specifications to understand testing performance analysis: U.S. Treasury bond futures are valued in tick sizes of $\frac{1}{32}$ (0.03125) of a point, each tick worth $31.25, so a full point (32 ticks) move of a contract is valued at $1,000 ($31.25 \times 32 =$ $1,000).

If bond futures move by $\frac{3}{32}$, for example, the contract value changes by $93.75 (three ticks multiplied by $31.25 = $93.75). If the bond futures rise by this amount and you are in a long position, $93.75 would thus be the unrealized gain, minus commissions and slippage. Similarly, if in a short position in a bond futures contract, this would be the amount of your loss. This is about all you need to understand for interpreting the results below. This market offers great potential for traders with a good trading system, as margin requirements are quite low for a one-lot (contract) position. This differs from stock index futures, where initial margin can be as high as $20,000 for the S&P 500. It is possible to trade bond futures, therefore, with as little as $2,500 per lot, although given performance data in the tables presented in this chapter, I assume a minimum account size of $5,000.

TABLE 12.1 Squeeze Play I Trading System Rules for Bond Futures (No Price Trigger)

Long Entry Signal	Short Entry Signal
Enter a long position on tomorrow's open when **EMA5-21** has crossed *from above to below* zero.	Enter a short position on tomorrow's open when **EMA5-21** had crossed *from below to above* zero.
Long Exit Signal	**Short Exit Signal**
Exit a long position on tomorrow's open when **EPC21-50** has crossed *from above to below* zero.	Exit a short position on tomorrow's open when **EPC21-50** had crossed *from below to above* zero.

In this chapter, I run Squeeze Play I on U.S. Treasury long bond futures. The rules for Squeeze Play I are presented in Table 12.1. First I apply the strategy without a price trigger, and then run tests again with the same price trigger used in the tests run on stock indices. Recall that Squeeze Play I employs two speeds, the EMA5-21 and EMA21-50. It signals a long trade when the faster EMA5-21 crosses *from above to below* zero. For short position entries, the EMA5-21 must cross *from below to above* zero to identify the sentiment conditions for a trade.

As for the trigger rules, trades are entered when the close today is higher than the previous day's high (for long position entries) and when the close today is lower than the previous day's low (for short position entries). While the same parameter settings are used for the sentiment waves that were run on stock indices, here I use a *normalized* put volume measure (instead of put/call contract volume ratio), which is a ratio of total long-bond futures put volume to total long-bond futures options volume, for the raw data. This helps to smooth the series, removing excess noise in the data. Additionally, I use a dollar value of options traded instead of options contract volume, which I have found works well in futures markets. Figure 12.1 shows the EMA21-50 plot of the series along with bond futures daily prices.

The performance results for Squeeze Play I (no triggers) tests on U.S. Treasury long bond futures are presented in Table 12.2. Total net profit is 24 points, or $24,000, which beats the buy-and-hold profit of 15.28 or $15, 280. The dates of this test are January 4, 1999 through November 26, 2003, with 1,788 days in the sample test period. There were a total of 30 trades, with an average profit of .44 points per trade ($440 dollars), an acceptable number in terms of transaction costs and potential slippage.

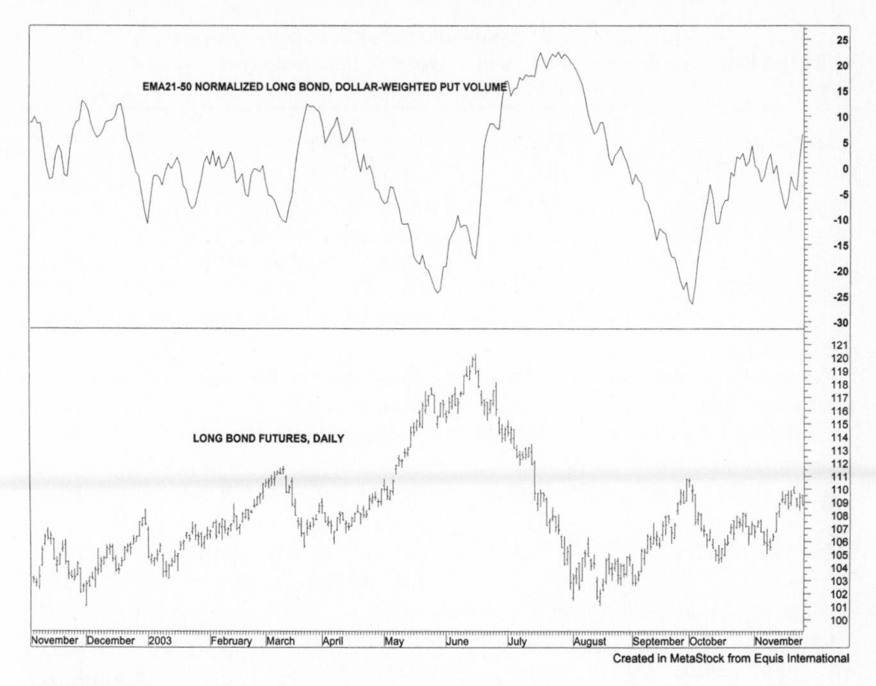

FIGURE 12.1 EMA21-50 plot with bond futures price. (*Source:* Pinnacle Data).

As for percentage gain, there are two ways to access the rate of return of this system. Typically, system traders using futures markets take the exchange minimum required to hold futures contract overnight and the open system drawdown amount as the initial investment to calculate rate of return. In this test and the one done with a price trigger in Table 12.3, however, I simply assume a \$5,000 initial investment, which is *higher* than minimum margin requirements combined with open system drawdown.

Unlike the testing on stocks, moreover, the system is not fully invested at all times. When a bond futures trade is closed (and any futures market tested in this book), for example, any profit or loss is tallied and added to the cumulative net total. When a new trade is entered, however, the position size is always the same: one contract. This is a limitation of the software used in testing, which does not permit any other money management approach. When testing stocks, recall that an initial investment of \$10,000 is not a constant value for each new trade entered. Instead, if a profit of

TABLE 12.2 Squeeze Play I on Bond Futures (without a Price Trigger) or Stops Using Normalized Dollar-Weighted Put Volume over Total Dollar-Weighted Options Volume

Total net profit	24.00	Largest win	4.75
Buy/Hold profit	15.28	Largest loss	-7.78
Days in test	1788	Average length of win	9.87
Total closed trades	55	Average length of loss	22.63
		Longest winning trade	30
Average profit per trade	0.44	Longest losing trade	46
		Most consecutive wins	8
Average Win/ Average Loss ratio	0.71	Most consecutive losses	2
Total long trades	27	Total bars out	562
Total short trades	28	Average length out	11.47
Winning long trades	19		
Winning short trades	20	System close drawdown	0.00
Total winning trades	39	Profit/Loss index	42.22
Total losing trades	16	System open drawdown	-0.37
		Reward/Risk index	98.46
Amount of winning trades	56.84		
Amount of losing trades	-32.84	Maximum open trade drawdown	-10.06
Average win	1.46		
Average loss	-2.05	Buy/Hold index	57.07

$5,000 was generated on the previous trade, the next trade investment is $15,000. And if the test is running on 50 percent margin, the next investment is $30,000—double the actual investment available for investing. Therefore, the results presented in Table 12.2 for bond futures do not reflect the full potential of this system. That said, based on an initial investment of $5,000, Squeeze Play I with no price triggers produced a total rate of return of 480 percent during the approximately 5-year study period, yielding an annualized return of 96 percent.

The overall profile of this performance is not great, but acceptable. An average win totaled 1.46 points, which was less than an average loss of –2.05, but with 71 percent of total trades being winners, the average-win-to-average-loss ratio is counterbalanced somewhat. The reward/risk ratio was excellent at 98.46, with no closed system drawdown, and just –.37 (–$370) for the open system drawdown. The maximum open trade drawdown is

TABLE 12.3 Squeeze Play I on Bond Futures with Price Trigger and No Stops Using Normalized Dollar-Weighted Put Volume over Total Dollar-Weighted Options Volume

Total net profit	27.47	Largest win	8.69
Buy/Hold profit	15.28	Largest loss	−2.50
Days in test	1,788	Average length of win	15.70
Total closed trades	29	Average length of loss	16.44
		Longest winning trade	60
Average profit per trade	0.95	Longest losing trade	28
Average Win/ Average Loss ratio	1.65	Most consecutive wins	7
Total long trades	19	Most consecutive losses	2
Total short trades	10	Total bars out	799
Winning long trades	11	Longest out period	105
Winning short trades	9		
Total winning trades	20	System close drawdown	0.00
Total losing trades	9	Profit/Loss index	72.71
		System open drawdown	−1.16
Amount of winning trades	37.78	Reward/Risk index	95.96
Amount of losing trades	−10.31		
Average win	1.89	Maximum open trade drawdown	−5.22
Average loss	−1.15	Buy/Hold index	79.77

large with −10 points, but as you will see shortly, the use of a price trigger substantially improves these key performance variables. Also, while not shown here, in-the-money bond futures options can be used as a surrogate, much like LEAPS on stocks, to improve performance.

Turning to the tests using the powerful price trigger, Table 12.3 presents test results showing significant improvements in key performance variables. Total net profit has increased to 27.47 points, with an accompanying fall in the maximum open trade drawdown to −5.22 points (almost half of the previous test level amount of −10.0). An average win compared to an average loss improves to a preferable number greater than 1.0—1.65, up from .71. The percentage of winning trades, finally, fell only slightly to 69 percent from 71 percent out of a total of 29 trades, 19 long and 10 short. Interestingly, short trades were 90 percent accurate (9 out of 10 were winners).

Considering profit rates in light of the non-trigger tests in Table 12.2, total return for the period increased from 480 percent to 549 percent, again assuming an initial account size of $5,000, which yields an annualized rate of return of 109 percent.

SUMMARY

Squeeze Play I with a price trigger has applications elsewhere as was demonstrated in this chapter with U.S. Treasury bond futures. Using a dollar-weighted normalized put volume as a sentiment measure of the options trading crowd—which helps remove unnecessary noise and may have applications on other futures markets—performance of the system tests were very good. The annualized rate of return registered 109 percent without any optimization. While not presented here, contract volume put/call ratios were also excellent in Squeeze Play I testing on bond futures.

CHAPTER 13

Option Implied Volatility and Investor Sentiment

As you will learn in this chapter, use of put and call *volume* is not the only way to measure the mood of the options trading crowd. Option *prices* also can provide valuable information about how bearish or bullish investor sentiment has become. Option prices can be used to calculate an *implied volatility* for any market. Levels of implied volatility may be thought of as what options traders are *expecting* volatility to be in the future; it depends partially on demand for put and call options in day-to-day trading. If traders are paying up for options then we know something about their emotional state.

In the previous chapters, I explained how options buyers tend to be wrong about their market views at extreme points, namely excessive levels of put or call buying, measured as a ratio of daily put and call contracts or dollar-weighted volume, and viewed in terms of sentiment waves, small and large. Here, instead of options volume data, the sentiment of options traders is assessed from what arguably is a purer source: the *prices paid for those options*, and how expensive or cheap these options have become. For example, an appetite for *expensive* options—not just *many* options—should tell us something about how much the crowd expects future prices to move, even if the crowd is not very good at predicting market direction. Interestingly, here options traders as a group also become useful from a contrarian point of view.

In order to understand how powerful implied volatility sentiment waves can be for contrarians and sentiment technicians, some background in options pricing theory is necessary. I have no intention of walking you through mathematical proofs, however, especially since I am not a mathematician and find the exercise pointless for purposes of trading crowd psychology. Nevertheless, I need to briefly explain both historical and implied volatility and how they are related. Once we know historical volatility, it is possible to obtain implied volatility of any option and then an average implied volatility measure for all the options in a particular market. This average number of implied volatility is one that we can plot historically and use in our trading systems.

THEORETICAL PRICING OF OPTIONS

Option pricing models, such as the widely used Black-Scholes model (and the Black model for futures options), use statistical or historical volatility as a variable to determine what an option price should be, given a number of other less important variables. Since historical (statistical) volatility is the most important variable in deriving the price of any out-of-the-money option, it follows that this should be well understood. Before discussing historical volatility, however, I want to mention two important related points.

First, I am not concerned with debates about the shortcomings of Black-Scholes or Black models that are the subject of so many academic articles. This has no relevance to how I use implied volatility data in the following chapter with trading systems. I accept these formulations for deriving implied volatility because I am looking at these in relation to previous levels generated by the *same* method (not compared with other methods). This makes debates about what constitutes real theoretical values of options—and hence accurate measures—of implied volatility a moot point for the purposes of trading systems presented in this book.

Another point I want to make here pertains to the measures of implied volatility I use for testing. For stock indices, I use the popular CBOE implied volatility stock indices, VXO and VIX, which are discussed shortly. For stock options volatility, meanwhile, I use a simple grand average of implied volatility of all stock options traded on that particular issue. Finally, I limit use of implied volatility to trading stocks and stock market indices only.

Stock and stock index options implied volatility has an inverse relationship, much like put/call ratios, to price stock movements. Therefore, if the S&P 500 falls on increasing bearish sentiment, implied volatility will rise and vice versa. Commodity futures options do not have this clear pattern, which is why use is restricted to stocks. Also, I lack accurate data for some markets, which is always a problem for back testing, so I stick to those markets where I have data that I can expect to be accurate (within some small margin of error).

With this understood, let's review some of the basic inferential methods for deriving historical volatility. First, what is meant by volatility? It is not uncommon to hear market commentators speak of stock market volatility. Typically, they are referring to erratic behavior of prices (up and down). This definition is actually somewhat misleading, however, since historical volatility has nothing do to with direction of the underlying, only how *large* these changes are and how quickly they are occurring.

Driving a car provides an excellent analogy for understanding historical volatility. When we take distance traveled divided by time of travel, we arrive at driving speed (in miles per hour). Historical volatility of a stock or stock futures is nothing more than the speed of price changes, but we measure it with a different gauge (annualized standard deviation of price changes). For example, using the auto analogy, if you are driving at 60 miles per hour and holding steady, the velocity is 60 miles traveled in one hour (60 mph). Price volatility, however, is not measured in hours but rather in years, or on an annualized percentage basis. For the volatility of an auto traveling at 60 miles per hour, therefore, we would have to know how many miles per year. In the case of the velocity of the auto traveling at 60 miles per hour, this turns out to be 525,600 miles per year.

But when speaking of stocks and stock futures, we need to convert this rate to a percentage, which is the way we can make easy comparisons with past levels and levels of historical volatility on other stocks and markets. So historical volatility of stocks and a stock index is actually a percentage number, like 20 or 25—sometimes higher, sometimes lower. This tells us how far the price will move, either up or down, one year ahead, just like the hourly rate of speed of an auto can be used to tell us how far we will travel in a year.

Historical volatility, as mentioned before, is the most important factor affecting an option's price. The Black-Scholes pricing model for options also uses time to expiration, price of the underlying in relation to the strike price, and short-term interest rates for the calculation. Historical volatility, however, can have the biggest impact. In the Black-Scholes model, volatility is an annualized standard deviation of price changes of the underlying, as alluded to above. Leaving aside technical issues related to the derivation of the historical deviation of price changes, the important point to grasp is that since historical volatility is a known number and it is the key factor in determining the level of option prices, any rise or fall will cause option prices to rise and fall, other things being equal. When stocks or a stock index rise, this is historically associated with falling historical volatility and when falling, rising historical volatility. This creates a pattern not unlike the behavior of put/call ratios.

Once calculated, historical volatility can be examined to see how volatile a stock, stock index, or commodity has been. This is easy to do because, based on the above calculation, we can compute the level of historical volatility as long as we have price data. Remember, historical volatility is calculated using daily price closes only. While uses of daily price closes may not be the best measure of volatility, it is the most popular method and the one I use here.

In plain English, if an asset's price tends to make larger daily price changes over a specified period of time in the past, historical volatility will be increasing. If price changes are smaller than the average of those in the recent past, then historical volatility will be decreasing. Again, this is an important point to keep in mind. Annualized historical volatility is computed without reference to the direction of the asset. Whether the stock or stock index price moves up or down is immaterial. It is just a question of by how much and how quickly. But since falling prices tend to experience larger daily ranges, historical volatility rises as stocks fall. And historical volatility rises and peaks at market bottoms, and falls to extreme lows at market tops, generally.

With this understanding of statistical volatility, we can begin to look at the more important concept of *imputed*, or *implied volatility*. Implied volatility is largely derived by using the actual price of the option and working backwards in the model. Instead of determining the theoretical price from historical volatility, we use the market price to work backwards solving for implied volatility. Essentially, if the market price is not equal to the theoretical price, then historical volatility is not equal to implied volatility. The difference between market and theoretical pricing is thus attributed to implied volatility.

This level of volatility meets the market expectation, as indicated by the market price of options in question or all the options on a particular stock or futures. If the market price is higher than the theoretical price, then the market is expecting higher volatility than recent historical volatility suggests. With stock options and stock indices, there is directional bias to levels of implied volatility; this means that higher levels suggest the options trading crowd has greater concern about market declines and lower levels imply complacency or less fear about potential for downside price movement. Panic demand for puts contributes to this dynamic.

Fortunately, implied volatility of stock index options is already calculated for us in the form of VIX and VXO indices. VIX and VXO are published daily by the CBOE and are widely quoted indicators measuring implied volatility for short-term, near-the-money options on the S&P 100 (VXO) and the S&P 500 (VIX). The same method can be applied to stocks, but I use a grand average method for stocks instead of the method used by the CBOE to calculate the VIX, VXO, and VXN (NASDAQ 100 implied volatility index). The data quality of these indices is excellent and there is a long data history for use in system testing, which makes them very attractive and valuable for system traders.

First we should take a look at the history of the VXO for S&P 100 (OEX) options. Known as the "fear gauge," it was created by Professor Robert Whaley of Duke University for the CBOE. Figures 13.1 and 13.2 plot the recent history of the VXO and VXN. As you can see, there is a clear pattern (the butterfly wings) in the relationship between the price series and the

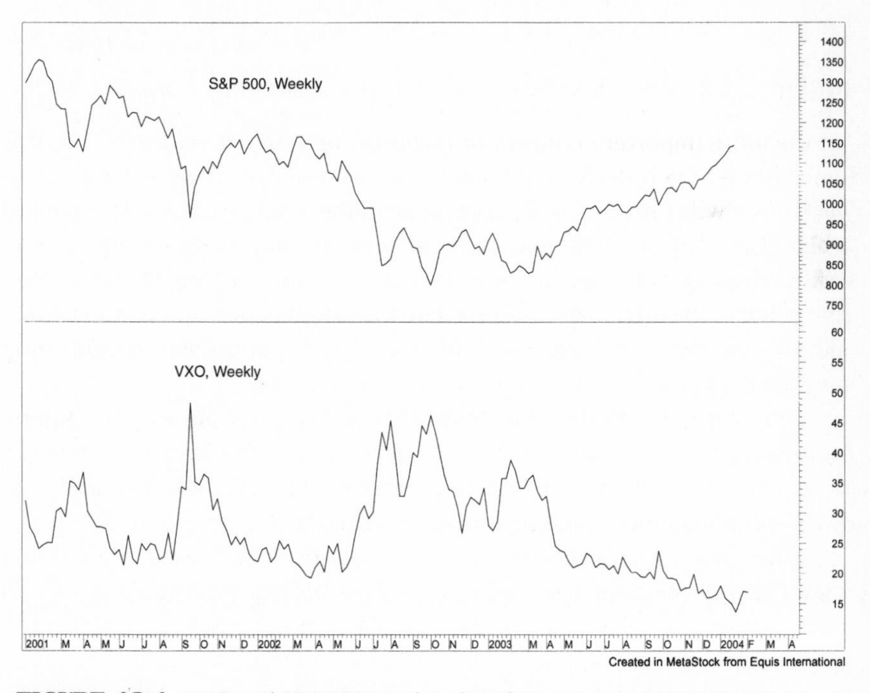

FIGURE 13.1 VXO and S&P 500 stock index chart. (*Source:* Pinnacle Data.)

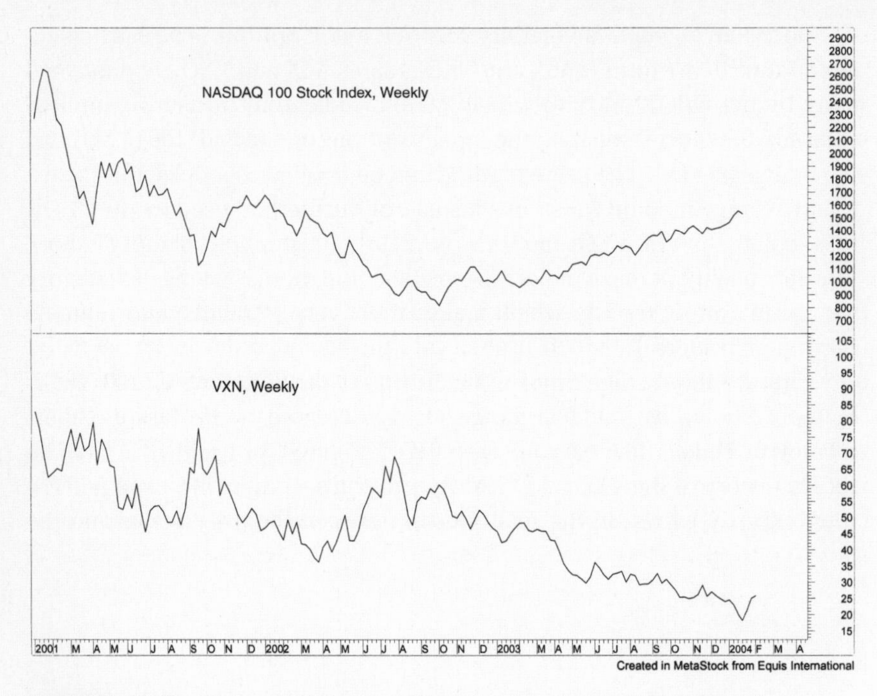

FIGURE 13.2 VXN and NASDAQ 100 stock index chart. (*Source:* Pinnacle Data.)

implied volatility series. As the market declines, VXO increases. Therefore, a high VXO represents increased fear that prices may decline more. A low VIX reading, however, indicates a complacency about potential risk to the downside. Contrarians interpret the latter as the sign of a nearby top in the market (too little fear), and the former as the indication of a bottom (too much fear). Later, I program this data to test this idea.

More recently, another stock market volatility index has become popular. Similar to the VXO and VIX, it is calculated for the NASDAQ 100 options, and is known as the VXN. The shorter history and lack of liquidity of NASDAQ 100 index options make VXN less useful.

When looking at implied volatilities of individual stock options, you can see the same contrarian pattern in many of the big-cap stocks traded on the market today. These typically have liquid options markets, which are required to calculate a valid reading of implied volatility. In the next two chapters, I use implied volatility for stock index options and big-cap stock options to test my Squeeze Play trading systems. The hope is that this sentiment data will work as well or even better than put/call ratios, signaling when the options trading crowd has begun to act as a misinformed group making shared miscalculations about future market direction.

SUMMARY

Like put/call ratios, options market prices provide valuable clues about crowd psychology. Too much implied volatility calculated from actual daily option prices tells us how fearful the crowd is at any point in time. Too little implied volatility tells us that the crowd has become complacent and, therefore, likely to be wrong at these extremes. Too much implied volatility indicates too much fear and thus the possibility of a market bottom. This chapter presents a nontechnical description of historical and implied volatility and how these price-driven dimensions of stock options and stock index options markets offer insight into investors' emotional state.

CHAPTER 14

Testing Option Volatility on Equity Indices

One key advantage to using implied volatility as a gauge of investor sentiment is that there can be no confusion about market sentiment. Prices are what they are, and inflated option premiums suggest that investors and traders typically expect more volatility. In the stock market, this usually occurs when fear is increasing and bearish sentiment is rising. Since there is an inverse relationship between implied volatility and stock market prices, this data provides sentiment technicians with a valuable trading tool. When the crowd gets too fearful or too fearless, once again, it is time to go against this sentiment.

Contrast the previous explanation with issues related to measures of the crowd using option volume, where it is not always clear what the volume represents. Is it opening or closing volume, short- or long-option volume, or is it volume from an option spread trade? Whether this unknown undermines performance when using put/call ratios is not clear. Using implied volatility, however, it is possible to skirt such issues.

In this chapter, I attempt to incorporate the implied volatility indices VXO (from S&P 100 options) and VIX (from S&P 500 options) into the trading systems developed and tested in previous chapters, but with some modifications. The VXN NASDAQ 100 implied volatility, meanwhile, is not used due to lack of liquidity in this market for options, which can distort levels of implied volatility.

The tests conducted in this chapter cover a longer time frame than those conducted in previous chapters. The sample period runs from December 25, 1995 through January 22, 2004. The actual testing period, however, is smaller because some of the moving averages used in the VXO and VIX sentiment oscillators require previous raw data to calculate a first data point, which reduces the test period by as much as 100 days in some of the tests.

The first system I test is Squeeze Play I, since it did so well on both equity indices and bond futures in previous testing. If I can achieve good results using implied volatility, then I can conclude this is an exceptionally robust trading system. The first test is on the S&P 500 stock index, and will be assumed to be traded with S&P 500 futures. I run the VXO first, which is based on implied volatility of S&P 100 options, not S&P 500 options, yet it should serve as a good proxy for stock market sentiment. Figure 14.1 provides a broad look at the cycles of investor fear and complacency captured by VXO implied volatility sentiment waves alongside movements of the S&P 500. These waves provide the initial screens for my Squeeze Play I trading system setup.

Table 14.1 shows the results of the first test, using Squeeze Play I, which are good, but not good enough, since the total net profit of 514.6

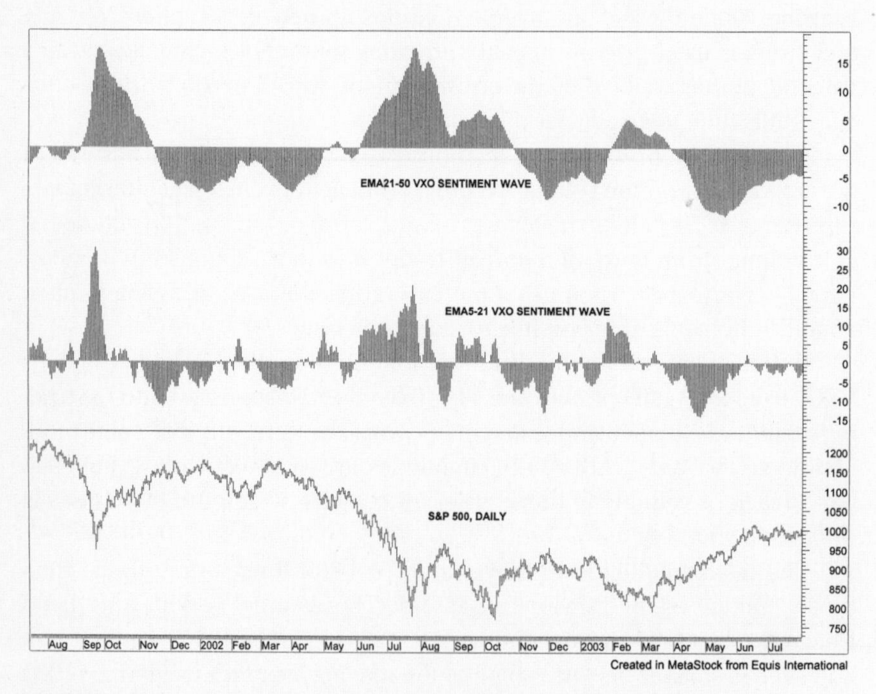

FIGURE 14.1 VXO sentiment waves and S&P 500. (*Source:* Pinnacle Data.)

TABLE 14.1 Squeeze Play I Test Using VXO on S&P 500

Total net profit	514.63	Largest win	432.13
Buy/Hold profit	680.62	Largest loss	-8.88
		Average length of win	21.00
Days in test	3,304	Average length of loss	23.33
Total closed trades	8	Longest winning trade	83
Average profit per trade	64.33	Longest losing trade	42
		Most consecutive wins	3
Average Win/Average Loss ratio	2.91	Most consecutive losses	2
		Total bars out	314
Total long trades	4	Average length out	34.89
		Longest out period	87
Total short trades	4	System close drawdown	0.00
		Profit/Loss index	79.35
Winning long trades	3		
Winning short trades	2	System open drawdown	-15.04
Total winning trades	5		
Total losing trades	3	Reward/Risk index	97.16
Amount of winning trades	648.57	Maximum open trade drawdown	-138.96
Amount of losing trades	-133.94	Buy/Hold index	-24.39
Average win	129.71		
Average loss	-44.65		

S&P 500 index points does not beat the buy-and-hold net profit of 680.62 index points, an essential benchmark for any trading system. Note, however, that overall performance is not so bad—which is a good sign. As you can see, in Table 14.1, the highest number of consecutive losses for this test period covering 3,304 days (about nine years) is just two, which speaks highly of the power of implied volatility to provide excellent timing signals. Also the reward/risk index is over 97, with no closed system drawdown. Other trading system test variables are excellent as well.

A closer look at the test results reveals that the system did not beat the buy-and-hold profit partly because there were just eight trades. Even with five of them winning, and an average-win-to-average-loss ratio at a fantastic 2.91, the small number of trades makes it difficult to pull enough points out the market to beat a buy-and-hold profit so large. Changes to some of the parameters might help, but I first test this system again using the VIX implied volatility measure, which is based upon premiums on S&P 500 options.

Table 14.2 shows the results of a rerun of Squeeze Play I on the S&P 500 using the VIX implied volatility index. Total net profit rises to 591.11 points, but still does not surpass the buy-and-hold net profit. Meanwhile, some of the system test variables deteriorate slightly, with closed-system drawdown going from zero to –65.22 points, and the average-win-to-average-loss ratio dropping to 2.01—still quite good. Interestingly, the total number of closed trades fell to six, with just one loser. Average wins easily beat average losses (131.27 points compared to 65.22).

TABLE 14.2 Squeeze Play I Test Using VIX on S&P 500

Total net profit	591.12	Largest win	428.41
Buy/Hold profit	680.62	Largest loss	−65.22
Days in test	3,304		
Total closed trades	6	Average length of win	20.80
Commissions paid	0.00	Average length of loss	33.00
Average profit per trade	98.52	Longest winning trade	84
		Longest losing trade	33
Average Win/Average Loss ratio	2.01	Most consecutive wins	5
		Most consecutive losses	1
Total long trades	2	Total bars out	347
		Average length out	57.83
Total short trades	4	Longest out period	83
		System close drawdown	−65.22
Winning long trades	2		
Winning short trades	3	Profit/Loss index	90.06
Total winning trades	5		
Total losing trades	1	System open drawdown	−80.26
Amount of winning trades	656.34	Reward/Risk index	88.05
Amount of losing trades	65.22	Maximum open trade drawdown	−76.70
Average win	131.27	Buy/Hold index	−13.15
Average loss	−65.22		

TABLE 14.3 EMA21-50 Squeeze Play II (Long/Short) at T + 30 Day Exits on S&P 500 (VIX)

Total net profit	848.93	Largest win	174.6
Buy/Hold profit	406.88	Largest loss	−124.55
Buy/Hold profit	2,577	Average length of win	32.00
Total closed trades	30	Average length of loss	32.00
Commissions paid	0.00	Longest winning trade	32
Average profit per trade	28.30	Longest losing trade	32
Average Win/Average Loss ratio	1.38	Most consecutive wins	8
		Most consecutive losses	3
Total long trades	13	Total bars out	875
		Average length out	28.23
Total short trades	17	Longest out period	170
		System close drawdown	−6.40
Winning long trades	9		
Winning short trades	11	Profit/Loss index	63.9
Total winning trades	20		
Total losing trades	10	System open drawdown	−27.45
Amount of winning trades	−479.69		
Average win	66.43	Reward/Risk index	96.87
Average loss	−47.97	Maximum open trade drawdown	−238.46
		Buy/Hold index	108.64

Now let's try running a modified Squeeze Play II, which worked well on stocks in Chapter 10 using put/call ratios. I only present the T + 30 time frame test results, but they all worked well in the testing. There were no stops used, and I have chosen the medium-speed oscillator to test first, the EMA21-50. After testing this faster oscillator, I conduct another round of tests with the EMA50-100, the slowest of the three oscillators used throughout this book, using Squeeze Play II system rules. Table 14.3 shows the results of Squeeze Play II using the EMA21-50 medium-speed oscillator. Clearly, use of Squeeze Play II dramatically improves results, well above buy-and-hold profit. Table 14.4 contains the rules for this system. Using VIX data first, total net profit jumps to 848.93 points, compared with buy-and-hold profit of 406.88. This yields a buy/hold index greater than 1.0, indicating

TABLE 14.4 EMA21-50 Squeeze Play II Rules—No Stops

EMA21-50 Squeeze Play II Rules—Entries	
Enter long position when **EMA21-50** highest high value in past 10 days is greater than +5 percent.	Enter short position when the **EMA21-50** lowest low value of the past 10 days is less than –5 percent.
EMA21-50 Squeeze Play II Rules—Exits	
Exit long position at T + 30-, T + 60-, and T + 90-day lagged periods from entry.	Exit short position at T + 30-, T + 60-, and T + 90-day lagged periods from entry.

more than double the buy/hold profit level. All the key system test variables are excellent, with a maximum of three consecutive losers, closed system drawdown of just –6.4 points, an average-win-to-average-loss ratio of 1.38, and a reward/risk index of 96.87. The only red flag is a maximum open trade drawdown of –238.46 points, which is quite large, even though the closed system drawdown is just –27.45.

Table 14.5 presents the results of the same system test using VXO. Here we get a slight deterioration in performance, with the total net profit falling to 812.69, although it is still more than double buy-and-hold profit. Even though the closed system drawdown drops to zero, other performance variables do not improve and some worsen. Curious about slower oscillator performance, I decided to run tests with EMA50-100 instead of EMA21-50. The results are presented in Tables 14.6 (VXO) and 14.8 (VIX).

Total profit (583.55) is lower, as seen in Table 14.6, but still beats buy-and-hold profit. Overall, there is not much change in performance. But substituting VIX for VXO and running the test again boosts total net profit to 804.97, as seen in Table 14.8.

The results seen in Table 14.8 have an excellent average-win-to-average-loss ratio of 1.85 (compared with 1.05 in the previous test). The reward/risk index registered 94.52 and maximum open-trade drawdown drops to –114.45, with a closed system drawdown of just –46.69 points.

By optimizing the price trigger rules, as seen in Table 14.7, which in these tests so far has been based on a closing price above the highest high or below the lowest low of the previous five days, results improve signifi-

TABLE 14.5 EMA21-50 Squeeze Play II (Long/Short) at T + 30-Day Exits on S&P 500 (VXO)

Total net profit	812.69	Largest win	156.68
Buy/Hold profit	406.20	Largest loss	-145.26
Days in test	2,577	Average length of win	62.00
Total closed trades	21	Average length of loss	62.00
Commissions paid	0.00	Longest winning trade	62
Average profit per trade	38.70	Longest losing trade	62
		Most consecutive wins	5
Average Win/Average Loss ratio	1.05	Most consecutive losses	2
		Total bars out	460
Total long trades	8	Average length out	20.91
Total short trades	13	Longest out period	170
		System close drawdown	0.00
Winning long trades	6	Profit/Loss index	61.96
Winning short trades	9		
Total winning trades	15	System open drawdown	-50.59
Total losing trades	6		
Amount of winning trades	1,311.70	Reward/Risk index	94.14
		Maximum open trade drawdown	-191.32
Amount of losing trades	-499.01	Buy/Hold index	165.41
Average win	87.45		
Average loss	-83.17		

cantly. Trying 0 through 10 days for highs and lows in an optimization routine reveals that all the combinations produced a net profit that beats buy-and-hold, with the best being a close above a 1 day high for longs and a close below an 8-day low for shorts. Highest net profit is 997.95, as shown in Table 14.9, which also lists all net profit associated with every possible combination of trigger parameters. It should be clear that acceptable profits are generated for all, with fewer number of days working best for longs and greater number of days best for short trades on average.

As a final test of implied volatility on equity indices, I sped up the oscillator to see if there is any profit potential in shorter cycles. The results are presented in Tables 14.10 and 14.11. Using a fast EMA1-10

TABLE 14.6 EMA50-100 Squeeze Play II (Long/Short) at T + 30-Day Exits on S&P 500 (VXO)

Total net profit	583.55	Largest win	161.39
Buy/Hold profit	406.20	Largest loss	−177.42
Days in test	2577	Average length of win	32.00
Total closed trades	25	Average length of loss	32.00
Commissions paid	0.00	Longest winning trade	32
Average profit per trade	23.34	Longest losing trade	32
		Most consecutive wins	7
Average Win/Average Loss ratio	1	Most consecutive losses	3
		Total bars out	961
Total long trades	12	Average length out	36.96
		Longest out period	223
Total short trades	13	System close drawdown	−29.01
Winning long trades	8	Profit/Loss index	53.14
Winning short trades	9		
Total winning trades	17	System open drawdown	−75.84
Total losing trades	8		
Amount of winning trades	1,098	Reward/Risk index	88.5
		Max open trade drawdown	−191.32
Amount of losing trades	−514.53		
Average win	64.59	Buy/Hold index	88.65
Average loss	−64.32		

oscillator, the system works on a simple threshold penetration rule, going long when the oscillator moves 5 percent above zero and short when it moves −5 percent below zero. Long and short trades are closed when the oscillator crosses zero. There are no stops or triggers used. A test using

TABLE 14.7 Modified EMA50-100 Squeeze Play II Price Trigger Rules

Enter long when today's closing price is greater than the highest high of the past *five* days.	Enter short when today's closing price is less than the lowest low of the past *five* days.

TABLE 14.8 EMA50-100 Squeeze Play II (Long/Short) at T + 30-Day Exits on S&P 500 (VIX)

Total net profit	804.97	Largest win	195.07
Buy/Hold profit	406.20	Largest loss	–88.60
Days in test	2,577		
Total closed trades	27	Average length of win	32.00
Commissions paid	0.00	Average length of loss	32.00
Average profit per trade	29.81	Longest winning trade	32
Average Win/Average Loss ratio	1.85	Longest losing trade	32
		Most consecutive wins	5
Total long trades	10	Most consecutive losses	2
		Total bars out	901
Total short trades	17	Average length out	32.18
		Longest out period	171
Winning long trades	8	System close drawdown	–46.69
Winning short trades	9		
Total winning trades	17	Profit/Loss index	68.21
Total losing trades	10		
Amount of winning trades	1,180.07	System open drawdown	–46.69
Amount of losing trades	–375.10	Reward/Risk index	94.52
Average win	69.42	Maximum open trade drawdown	–114.45
Average loss	–37.51	Buy/Hold index	160.23

VXO on the OEX produced 488 points of net profit compared with buy-and-hold profit of 208.6, which is quite good. Performance overall was mixed, however, as seen in Table 14.10. For example, there were seven consecutive losers and average wins do not beat average losses, but reward/risk was excellent at 99.05.

Running the same test on the S&P 500 using VIX, total net profit was 859.9 with a better overall profile, and certainly acceptable as a trading system. Notably, maximum consecutive losses drop to four. If using S&P futures with an initial account balance of $25,000, rate of return was 95 percent annually.

TABLE 14.9 EMA50-100 Squeeze Play II (Long/Short) at T + 30 Day Exits on S&P 500 (VIX). Optimized Triggers 0–10 Run with VIX. Long trades did better with lower price trigger parameter values and short trades showed best performance with higher parameter values.

Test #	Net Profit	Total Trades	Winning	Losing	Average Win/ Average Loss	Opt: Long Trigger	Opt: Short Trigger	Test #
90	997.9497	25	18	7	1.8904	1	8	90
94	975.3599	24	17	7	2.4007	5	8	94
68	968.2698	26	19	7	1.4938	1	6	68
79	957.3497	26	19	7	1.4335	1	7	79
91	913.8496	25	18	7	1.6197	2	8	91
101	903.2898	24	17	7	1.8508	1	9	101
72	893.6	25	17	8	1.9847	5	6	72
46	892.1301	28	21	7	1.0635	1	4	46
116	888.6599	21	16	5	2.1257	5	10	116
83	885.3798	25	17	8	1.8979	5	7	83
69	884.1697	26	19	7	1.3065	2	6	69
105	880.7	23	16	7	2.3456	5	9	105
13	874.7099	29	20	9	1.2921	1	1	13
80	873.2496	26	19	7	1.2586	2	7	80
39	868.5402	27	19	8	1.5235	5	3	39
57	862.84	28	19	9	1.4601	1	5	57
112	862.4098	23	16	7	1.8973	1	10	112
14	851.0798	28	20	8	1.1323	2	1	14
24	850.1701	29	21	8	1.0776	1	2	24
35	841.9301	29	20	9	1.2621	1	3	35
28	836.7902	27	20	7	1.2372	5	2	28
47	835.67	28	21	7	0.97	2	4	47
50	834.2603	27	19	8	1.3756	5	4	50

Test #	Net Profit	Total Trades	Winning	Losing	Average Win/ Average Loss	Opt: Long Trigger	Opt: Short Trigger	Test #
25	826.54	28	21	7	0.9292	2	2	25
102	819.1897	24	17	7	1.58	2	9	102
36	818.3	28	20	8	1.1054	2	3	36
58	806.3798	28	19	9	1.3328	2	5	58
61	804.9701	27	17	10	1.8506	5	5	61
17	796.05	27	19	8	1.491	5	1	17
42	779.31	26	17	9	1.5673	8	3	42
113	778.3097	23	16	7	1.6168	2	10	113
31	774.4301	26	18	8	1.3772	8	2	31
43	763.2302	26	16	10	1.7577	9	3	43
119	762.1599	21	15	6	2.1692	8	10	119
32	758.3502	26	17	9	1.5519	9	2	32
92	755.4497	25	16	9	1.6915	3	8	92
97	754.2	23	15	8	2.3527	8	8	97
108	754.2	23	15	8	2.3527	8	9	108
95	748.3799	23	15	8	2.2808	6	8	95
120	746.0801	21	14	7	2.4036	9	10	120
117	743.9799	21	15	6	2.0566	6	10	117
41	742.5202	26	16	10	2.0284	7	3	41
98	738.1201	23	14	9	2.5817	9	8	98
109	738.1201	23	14	9	2.5817	9	9	109
106	736.02	23	15	8	2.2519	6	9	106
20	727.8699	26	17	9	1.5095	8	1	20
40	725.4802	26	17	9	1.6017	6	3	40
96	722.0199	23	14	9	2.543	7	8	96
118	717.6199	21	14	7	2.3352	7	10	118
21	711.79	26	16	10	1.6923	9	1	21

TABLE 14.9 *(Continued)*

Test #	Net Profit	Total Trades	Winning	Losing	Average Win/ Average Loss	Opt: Long Trigger	Opt: Short Trigger	Test #
30	710.7701	26	17	9	1.673	7	2	30
107	709.6599	23	14	9	2.5104	7	9	107
93	705.6498	25	16	9	1.4939	4	8	93
29	693.7302	26	18	8	1.3091	6	2	29
99	690.33	22	14	8	1.8653	10	8	99
121	685.93	20	14	6	1.5764	10	10	121
19	680.27	26	16	10	1.9868	7	1	19
110	677.97	22	14	8	1.8421	10	9	110
70	673.6899	26	16	10	1.5562	3	6	70
73	672.5801	24	15	9	1.9265	6	6	73
114	668.7498	22	15	7	1.4193	3	10	114
81	665.4697	26	16	10	1.5169	3	7	81
75	664.2199	24	15	9	1.8812	8	6	75
86	664.2199	24	15	9	1.8812	8	7	86
18	663.23	26	17	9	1.5629	6	1	18
51	661.7903	26	17	9	1.4175	6	4	51
103	660.7898	24	15	9	1.6534	3	9	103
84	658.3999	24	15	9	1.8407	6	7	84
53	658.03	26	17	9	1.3809	8	4	53
76	648.1401	24	14	10	2.0974	9	6	76
87	648.1401	24	14	10	2.0974	9	7	87
74	646.22	24	14	10	2.1564	7	6	74
44	642.7504	25	16	9	1.3496	10	3	44
54	641.9502	26	16	10	1.5521	9	4	54
52	635.4303	26	16	10	1.5928	7	4	52

Test #	Net Profit	Total Trades	Winning	Losing	Average Win/ Average Loss	Opt: Long Trigger	Opt: Short Trigger	Test #
62	632.5002	26	15	11	1.8884	6	5	62
85	632.0399	24	14	10	2.0649	7	7	85
48	625.1901	28	18	10	1.1959	3	4	48
64	624.14	26	15	11	1.8539	8	5	64
71	623.89	26	16	10	1.4018	4	6	71
115	618.9498	22	15	7	1.232	4	10	115
82	615.6697	26	16	10	1.3705	4	7	82
77	614.5302	23	14	9	1.6806	10	6	77
33	611.0003	25	17	8	1.0987	10	2	33
104	610.9899	24	15	9	1.4602	4	9	104
65	608.0602	26	14	12	2.0634	9	5	65
63	606.1401	26	14	12	2.1017	7	5	63
55	603.7404	25	16	9	1.2836	10	4	55
88	600.35	23	14	9	1.6202	10	7	88
37	598.7001	28	17	11	1.328	3	3	37
38	598.7001	28	17	11	1.328	4	3	38
59	595.9	28	16	12	1.5633	3	5	59
22	580.5002	25	16	9	1.3031	10	1	22
26	577.9401	28	18	10	1.1215	3	2	26
27	577.9401	28	18	10	1.1215	4	2	27
49	575.3902	28	18	10	1.0953	4	4	49
66	574.4503	25	14	11	1.7299	10	5	66
60	546.1	28	16	12	1.4334	4	5	60
15	518.9199	28	17	11	1.2364	3	1	15
16	518.9199	28	17	11	1.2364	4	1	16

TABLE 14.10 EMA1-10 5% Trading System on OEX with VXO

Total net profit	488.04	Largest win	37.44
Buy/Hold profit	208.65		
Days in test	2,577	Largest loss	–66.26
Total closed trades	185		
Commissions paid	0.00	Average length of win	5.36
Average profit per trade	2.66	Average length of loss	10.72
Average Win/Average Loss ratio	0.89	Longest winning trade	21
		Longest losing trade	41
Total long trades	85	Most consecutive wins	8
		Most consecutive losses	7
Total short trades	100	Total bars out	750
		Average length out	5.21
Winning long trades	60	Longest out period	19
Winning short trades	58	System close drawdown	0.00
Total winning trades	118	Profit/Loss index	35.99
Total losing trades	67		
Amount of winning trades	1,360	System open drawdown	–4.705
		Reward/Risk index	99.05
Amount of losing trades	–868.18	Maximum open trade drawdown	–85.70
Average win	11.53		
Average loss	–12.96	Buy/Hold index	132.02

TABLE 14.11 EMA1-10 5% Trading System on SP500 with VIX

Total net profit	859.91	Largest win	72.32
Buy/Hold profit	406.88	Largest loss	–136.46
Days in test	2,577	Average length of win	5.73
Total closed trades	185	Average length of loss	10.14
Commissions paid	0.00	Longest winning trade	29
Average profit per trade	4.69	Longest losing trade	41
Average Win/Average Loss ratio	0.85	Most consecutive wins	8
		Most consecutive losses	4
Total long trades	85	Total bars out	750
		Average length out	5.21
Total short trades	100	Longest out period	19
		System close drawdown	0.00
Winning long trades	59	Profit/Loss index	34.35
Winning short trades	60		
Total winning trades	119	System open drawdown	–9.53
Total losing trades	66	Reward/Risk index	98.90
Amount of winning trades	2,511	Maximum open trade drawdown	–167.78
Amount of losing trades	–1,643.25	Buy/Hold index	109.43
Average win	21.10		
Average loss	–24.90		

SUMMARY

Using a EMA21-50 medium speed and EMA50-100 slow-speed oscillator in Squeeze Play II, and a faster EMA1-10 oscillator in a simple 5 percent extreme threshold penetration system, this chapter shows that implied volatility offers another profitable way to trade against the crowd. Testing was conducted on the S&P 500 and S&P 100 equity indices using CBOE's new and old implied volatility indices VIX (for S&P 500) and VXO (for S&P 100). VIX and VXO indices are calculated based on options that trade on these indices and provide a gauge of excessive fear and greed. As the tests show, if you go against the crowd during times of high levels of fear or times of too much complacency, by using implied volatility as a measure of these moods, excellent profits are obtainable. In the next chapter, I apply similar tests to stocks to see if these results can be reproduced.

CHAPTER 15

Stock Options Volatility and Sentiment Long Waves

As you've seen, implied volatility provides a psychological gauge that offers tremendous profit potential if properly analyzed and processed. In this chapter, I extend this sentiment approach to individual stocks.

Let's quickly review the trading setups I use in this chapter. A version of Squeeze Play II trading rules is applied in the same manner used in Chapter 14. Once again, the logic is based on finding entries that are triggered by price action immediately following periods of above-average bullish or bearish sentiment. A long position is signaled when the EMA21-50 oscillator's (running on daily stock option implied volatility data now) highest high value in the past 10 days is greater than 5 percent, and when today's close is greater than yesterday's high. A short position is established when the EMA21-50 oscillator's lowest low value in the past 10 days is less than –5 percent, and when today's close is less than yesterday's low.

For the exit plan, I again use the T + 30-, T + 60-, and T + 90-day triple-exit approach used successfully with put/call ratios and with implied volatility in Chapter 14 trading the equity indices. I assess this strategy, moreover, in terms of a LEAPS and non-LEAPS approach, to again illustrate the power of using options to capture the long-term swings in price.

Just like stock index options, individual stock options provide the pricing information needed to derive implied volatility. However, the average implied volatility calculation for stock options is not that which is used to calculate the VIX, VXN, and VXO looked at in the previous chapter. It is possible, however, to obtain the same data from certain vendors if the other VIX-like calculations were preferred. Here we simply take a daily grand

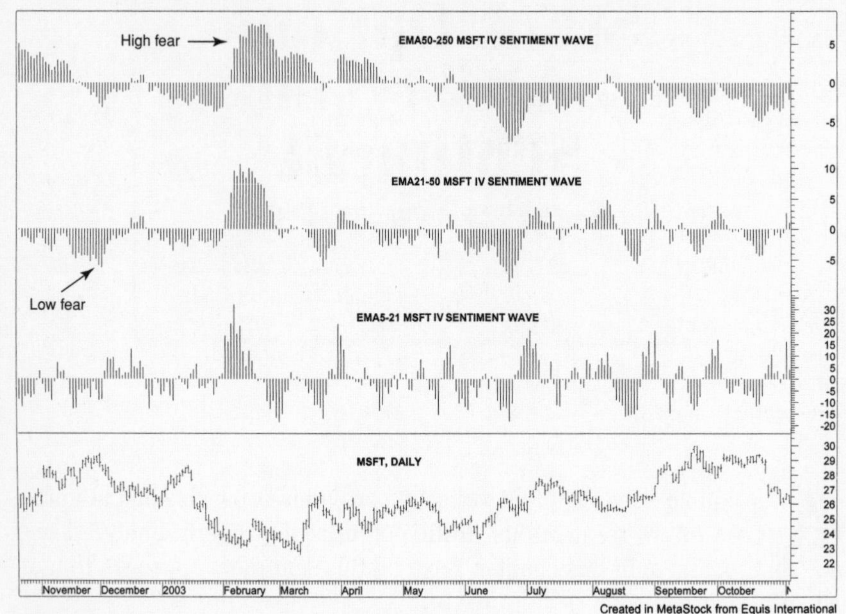

FIGURE 15.1 MSFT implied volatility sentiment waves.

average of implied volatility calculated from all of a stock's options to use as a gauge of options market sentiment. For our purposes, this provides a good enough sentiment measure, as you can see in Figure 15.1. Again, like with VIX and VXO, a high reading indicates expensive options and is a condition that arises near market bottoms; a low reading is typically associated with market tops when there is low volatility and less fear. If the crowd is getting it wrong at these sentiment extremes (the overall assumption throughout this book), then a trading system built using this data should provide reasonably good trading results.

Let's look at our same group of stocks to test this idea: Microsoft, IBM, Citigroup, Wal-Mart, GE, and Merck. Before we evaluate the individual and group performance of these groups, however, I want to illustrate the power of sentiment information by running the system with the price triggers only first. Tables 15.1 and 15.2 show IBM T + 30 Squeeze Play II test results *without* a sentiment screen, using just a close above the previous day's high as a long position entry signal and a close below the previous day's low as a short

TABLE 15.1 Squeeze Play II—IBM (No Sentiment Screen, Longs Only, T + 30)

Total net profit	–$2,085.83	Average win	$2,064.38
Percent gain/loss	–20.86	Average loss	–$2,917.03
Annual percent gain/loss	–3.54	Largest win	$7,868.77
		Largest loss	–$14,388.00
Initial investment	$10,000.00	Average length of win	32.00
Buy/Hold profit	$14,205.71	Average length of loss	32.00
Days in test	2,150	Longest winning trade	32
Buy/Hold percentage gain/loss	142.06	Longest losing trade	32
Annual Buy/Hold percentage gain/loss	24.12	Most consecutive wins	4
		Most consecutive losses	4
Total closed trades	40	Total bars out	1,470
Commissions paid	0.00	Average length out	35.85
Average profit per trade	–$52.72	Longest out period	44
Average Win/Average Loss ratio	0.71	System close drawdown	–$5,690.10
Total long trades	40	Profit/Loss index	–4.21
Total short trades	0	System open drawdown	–$7,607.69
Winning long trades	23	Reward/Risk index	–27.42
Winning short trades	0	Maximum open trade drawdown	–$16,170.60
Total winning trades	23		
Total losing trades	17	Buy/Hold index	–114.52
Amount of winning trades	$47,480.82		
Amount of losing trades	–$49,589.53		

position entry signal. Not surprisingly, both test results show net losses, with longs losing $2,085.83 and shorts losing $7,474.63. Once the sentiment rules are dropped into the trading system, however, the equity performance gets a facelift. Tables 15.3 and 15.4 show the long and short position tests for the T + 30 exit time frame only.

Profits on the long side jump amazingly to $35,957.30 and on the short side to $5,247.63, compared with a buy-and-hold profit of $14,205.71. For the longs, the annual percent gain is 61.04 percent compared with a buy-

TABLE 15.2 Squeeze Play II—IBM (No Sentiment Screen, Shorts Only, T + 30)

Total net profit	–$7,474.63	Average win	$270.07
Percent gain/loss	–74.75	Average loss	–$573.00
		Largest win	$1,126.52
Annual percent gain/loss	–12.69	Largest loss	–$2,062.44
Initial investment	$10,000.00	Average length of win	32.00
		Average length of loss	32.00
Buy/Hold profit	$14,205.71	Longest winning trade	32
Days in test	2,150	Longest losing trade	32
Buy/Hold percentage gain/loss	142.06		
Annual Buy/Hold percent gain/loss	24.12	Most consecutive wins	4
		Most consecutive losses	4
Total closed trades	41	Total bars out	1,441
Commissions paid	0.00	Average length out	34.31
Average profit per trade	–$182.31	Longest out period	48
Average Win/Average Loss ratio	0.47	System close drawdown	–$8,944.86
Total long trades	0	Profit/Loss index	–59.29
Total short trades	41	System open drawdown	–$10,000.00
		Reward/Risk index	–74.75
Winning long trades	0	Maximum open trade drawdown	–$2,062.44
Winning short trades	19		
Total winning trades	19	Buy/Hold index	–152.62
Total losing trades	22		
Amount of winning trades	$5,131.32		
Amount of losing trades	–$12,605.95		

and-hold gain of 24.12 percent. Combining sentiment screens with price-based triggers clearly enables traders to capture tremendous profit, well above buy-and-hold, something that has been repeatedly demonstrated throughout this book. The problem, of course, is getting enough good performance from all the stocks in a group. There are likely to be underperformers or even losers, as seen previously. One issue worth noting here is that while many of the system tests show inferior performance in terms of the buy-and-hold approach, there are generally few actual losing system tests showing absolute losses (as opposed to relative losses from not beating buy-and-hold). This is true in most of the tests throughout this book.

TABLE 15.3 Squeeze Play II—IBM (with Sentiment Screen, Longs Only, T + 30)

Total net profit	$35,957.30	Average win	$5,883.44
Percent gain/loss	359.57		
		Average loss	–$2,832.28
Annual percent gain/loss	61.04		
		Largest win	$18,207.20
Initial investment	$10,000.00	Largest loss	–$7,411.09
Buy/Hold profit	$14,205.71	Average length of win	32.00
Days in test	2,150	Average length of loss	32.00
Buy/Hold percentage gain/loss	142.06	Longest winning trade	32
Annual Buy/Hold percentage gain/loss	24.12	Longest losing trade	32
		Most consecutive wins	4
Total closed trades	15	Most consecutive losses	3
Commissions paid	0.00	Total bars out	1,467
Average profit per trade	2,397.15	Average length out	91.69
Average Win/Average Loss ratio	2.08	Longest out period	196
		System close drawdown	0.00
Total long trades	15	Profit/Loss index	67.91
Total short trades	0	System open drawdown	0.00
		Reward/Risk index	100.00
Winning long trades	9	Maximum open trade drawdown	–$11,811.06
Winning short trades	0		
Total winning trades	9	Buy/Hold index	153.12
Total losing trades	6		
Amount of winning trades	$52,950.99		
Amount of losing trades	–$16,993.69		

TABLE 15.4 Squeeze Play II—IBM (with Sentiment Screen, Shorts Only, T + 30)

Total net profit	$5,247.63	Average win	$1,439.13
Percent gain/loss	52.48	Average loss	–$1,540.90
Annual percent gain/loss	9.05	Largest win	$3,875.51
		Largest loss	–$3,155.76
Initial investment	$10,000.00		
		Average length of win	32.00
Buy/Hold profit	$14,205.71	Average length of loss	32.00
Days in test	2,150	Longest winning trade	32
Buy/Hold percentage gain/loss	24.12	Longest losing trade	32
Annual Buy/Hold percentage gain/loss	24.12	Most consecutive wins	3
		Most consecutive losses	2
Total closed trades	14	Total bars out	1,473
Commissions paid	0.00	Average length out	98.20
Average profit per trade	$374.83	Longest out period	249
Average Win/Average Loss ratio	0.93	System close drawdown	–$5,571.78
Total long trades	0	Profit/Loss index	40.52
Total short trades	14	System open drawdown	–$6,672.47
Winning long trades	0	Reward/Risk index	44.02
Winning short trades	9	Maximum open trade drawdown	–$3,868.15
Total winning trades	9		
Total losing trades	5	Buy/Hold index	–60.75
Amount of winning trades	$12,952.13		
Amount of losing trades	–$7,704.51		

When comparing the group performance (our six stocks) using implied volatility oscillators to put/call ratio test results, the latter show superior performance. Table 15.5 contains the results previously presented and Tables 15.6 and 15.7 show non-LEAPS and LEAPS results running with implied volatility. The long LEAPS trades, where the best performance usually appears, show $93,246.60 for T + 30 net profit using implied volatility compared with $148,434 for Squeeze Play II put/call ratio system tests.

TABLE 15.5 Squeeze Play II Performance—LEAPS Options Using T + 30 Through T + 90 Time Frames as Exits (Put/Call Ratios)

	T + 30 Longs	T + 60 Longs	T + 90 Longs	T + 30 Shorts
IBM	$37,135.83	$19,869.53	$48,302.92	29322.19
C	20702.51	795.86	2035.06	−3077.04
MRK	2327.06	5630.18	6350.77	32836.79
WMT	26232.69	29283	39843.60	−1374.42
GE	−3616.97	1052.41	7690.51	5145.82
MSFT	65653.25	47152.64	80943.01	−3988.93
TOTAL	148,434.40	103,783.60	185,165.90	60,238.83

	T + 60 Shorts	T + 90 Shorts	Total Profit	Buy/Hold Profit
IBM	9933.41	4140.41	148,704.30	38,150.67
C	4140.90	2422.69	27,019.98	35,108.10
MRK	20516.44	12228.17	79,889.41	5,028.65
WMT	−3117.79	−2268.77	89,972.73	115,429.15
GE	15874.54	1822.13	27,968.44	11,213.29
MSFT	812.29	−2869.02	187,703.20	85,447.55
TOTAL	48,159.79	15,475.61	561,258.10	$290,377.41

The best results for implied volatility were for the T + 90 longs-only time frame, which produced a net profit of $81,212.35, but this was still substantially below the $185,165.90 produced using the same strategy with put/call ratios. However, total long trades did produce a profit of $223,476.17 for the LEAPS approach! Short trades showed sharply deteriorating performance, with only T + 30 showing a small profit for the non-LEAPS approach. This improves from $2,250 to $15,676 with the LEAPS plan, but well below profits produced using put/call ratios for T + 30 shorts-only trades, a profit of $60,238.90.

Finally, the tests using implied volatility showed substantially less total net profit, with $104,300.00 for the non-LEAPS approach, and $228,654 for LEAPS-option trading on the trade signals from Squeeze Play II, as seen in Tables 15.6 and 15.7. Contrast this with Squeeze Play II results using put/call ratios, which made a total of $561,258.10, well above buy/hold profits. This is well above the $290,377.41 in buy/hold total profit for the group.

TABLE 15.6 EMA21-50 Squeeze Play II Performance—No Stops Using T + 30 Through T + 90 Time Frames as Exits (Implied Volatility)

	T + 30 Longs	T + 60 Longs	T + 90 Longs	T + 30 Shorts
IBM	$35,957.30	$11,723.53	$44,449.87	$5,247.63
C	–$1,896.43	–$4,210.59	–$3,268.80	–$2,913.50
MRK	$5,995.33	–$5,285.83	–$3,075.28	$8,105.82
WMT	$22,399.14	$13,300.53	$28,715.99	–$5,534.29
GE	$1,364.24	–$5,857.54	$2,194.04	$2,632.71
MSFT	$10,902.43	$7,011.32	–$6,589.77	–$5,288.23
TOTAL	$74,722.01	$16,681.42	$62,426.05	$2,250.14

	T + 60 Shorts	T + 90 Shorts	Total Profit	Buy/Hold Profit
IBM	–$3,375.87	–$5,179.64	$88,822.82	38,150.67
C	–$4,210.59	–$4,279.97	–$20,779.90	35,108.10
MRK	–$216.35	–$4,432.59	$1,091.10	5,028.65
WMT	–$7,643.91	–$7,803.44	$43,434.02	115,429.15
GE	$1,232.32	–$1,994.29	–$428.52	11,213.29
MSFT	–$6,442.50	–$7,429.80	–$7,836.55	85,447.55
TOTAL	–$20,657.00	–$31,119.70	$104,303.00	290,377.41

TABLE 15.7 EMA10-21 Squeeze Play II Performance—LEAPS Options Using T + 30 Through T + 90 Time Frames as Exits (Implied Volatility)

	T + 30 Longs	T + 60 Longs	T + 90 Longs	T + 30 Shorts
IBM	$40,053.01	$16,864.39	$44,449.87	$7,880.84
C	$1,054.31	–$1,763.93	–$3,268.80	–$2,077.79
MRK	$9,535.21	–$1,304.99	–$3,075.28	$11,510.21
WMT	$22,507.63	$18,004.96	$28,715.99	–$2,440.34
GE	$4,015.15	–$1,526.03	$5,920.74	$2,632.71
MSFT	$16,081.29	$18,742.82	$8,469.83	–$1,829.18
TOTAL	$93,246.60	$49,017.22	$81,212.35	$15,676.45

	T + 60 Shorts	T + 90 Shorts	Total Profit	Buy/Hold Profit
IBM	–$767.03	–$1,600.80	$106,880.28	38,150.67
C	–$1,763.93	–$2,521.02	–$10,341.16	35,108.10
MRK	–$216.35	–$1,668.49	$14,780.31	5,028.65
WMT	–$3,563.53	–3,964.56	$63,224.71	115,429.15
GE	$4,160.91	$2,764.08	$17,967.56	11,213.29
MSFT	–$2,322.25	–$2,999.59	$36,142.92	85,447.55
TOTAL	–$4,472.18	–$6,025.82	$228,654.61	290,377.41

SUMMARY

The tests in this chapter that use stock options implied volatility in LEAPS and non-LEAPS Squeeze Play II produced profitable results for all long time frames. Taking overall profitability for the group, Squeeze Play II did not beat the buy-and-hold profit, and fell far short of performance derived from using this same system with put/call ratio data. This hardly represents the final word on stock options implied volatility, since there are other ways to both calculate this sentiment gauge and to trade it. The results derived here with Squeeze Play II at least suggest that these secondary data streams lack the predictive power that contract volume has been shown to have, at least at the level of individual stocks. However, those clever enough may find better ways to collect and process this data.

CHAPTER 16

Gauging Crowd Psychology with Short Selling Ratios

Short selling is a bet on an expected market decline, or fall of an individual stock, by selling stock that is borrowed. In the case of a commodity, there is no borrowing, just short sales, but the same profit/loss dynamics exist. Stock short sellers are required to return the stock that was borrowed to the broker at a later date. Therefore, if the market that is shorted declines, a trader or investor buys back the shares sold short at a lower price and thus at a profit (sold high, bought low), at which point the shares are returned to the broker.

If all this sounds confusing, it actually happens automatically with orders to either "get short," (a click of the mouse in today's online trading environment), or to "cover-buy," the term used to explain when shorts buy back, or "offset" their open short positions. Since open short positions (known as short interest) reflect shares that have not yet been repurchased but need to be eventually, they ultimately represent potential buying power. In this and the following chapter, I show how to quantify this short-selling activity with the right data in order to objectively trade against this crowd using mechanical trading systems.

One of the oldest and most useful measures of investor sentiment, short-selling activity on Wall Street has proved to be a very reliable market-timing tool for stock market sentiment technicians. Figure 16.1 shows the steady growth in short sale activity by one of the most important players on Wall Street, the so-called smart money specialists, who are members of the exchange authorized to make the market in particular stocks. While many have tried to use this series in relation to the public short sales—seen in Figure 16.2—or on its own to time the market, this ratio has become problematic for a number of reasons.

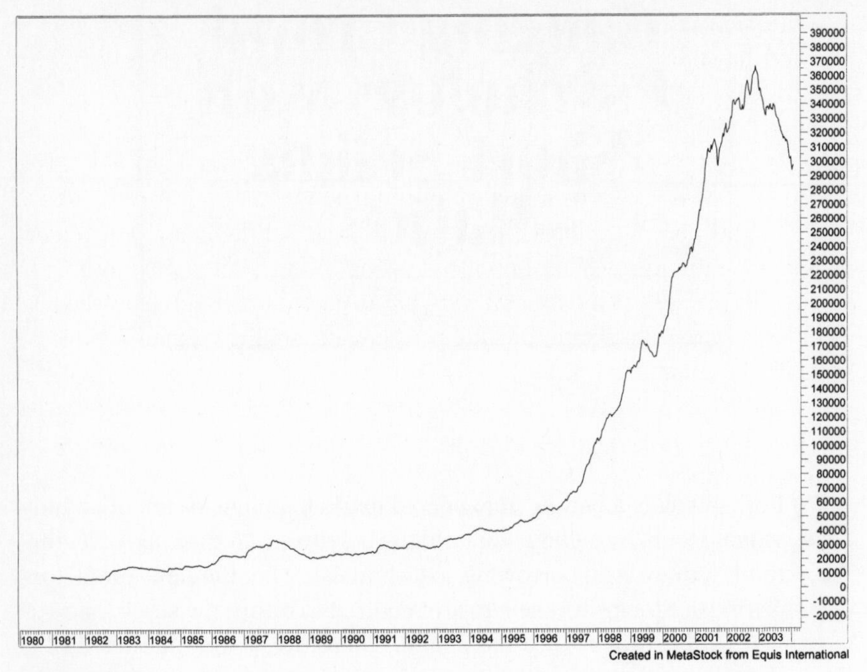

FIGURE 16.1 Total NYSE weekly specialist short sales. (*Data Source:* Pinnacle Data.)

THE PUBLIC GETS MORE INVOLVED IN SHORT SELLING

With click-and-point ease, traders can "get short" a stock or futures market without much trouble (although not all stocks are available for shorting) in today's online trading environment. But there are certain rules about when exactly a stock can be shorted (a point discussed in more detail below). Since shorting a stock reflects bearish expectations, data showing *increasing* short-selling intensity indicates the crowd is becoming more bearish. This is especially the case when unprofessional short selling activity (the public shorts) increases, as opposed to total short selling going on at any one time, by NYSE floor traders, specialists, and other members of the exchange (the professional or so-called "smart money"). My favorite short-selling ratio is one that takes a little effort to calculate but provides excellent signals; it provides a reading of public shorting activity only, which history shows is one of the best indicators of the wrong-headed crowd.

In the past 20 years, traders and investors have become more actively involved in short-selling activity. Figure 16.2 demonstrates this trend, with a chart of total public short-selling activity. This trend in the data can be seen rising sharply in the late 1990s. However, since total NYSE volume was also trending higher during the same period, this trend in total public shorting does not give us a picture of the true magnitude of public short-selling sentiment. Just how much public short-selling sentiment occurs depends on the ratio of total public shorting to the total volume of stocks traded. To process this data in a way that is useful for trading, however, it is necessary to take a ratio of total public short-selling volume divided by total NYSE volume.

Figure 16.3 provides a view of this normalized public short sales series (which has also been detrended using a difference of four- and eight-week exponential moving averages). The oscillations clearly show a very nice pattern of the public at increased shorting extremes just when the S&P 500 is ready to put in a bottom. The same is true for market tops when public short-selling activity is at an extreme low. This is similar behavior, therefore, to our options crowd, which gets it wrong generally at market sentiment extremes, as measured in our put/call ratios and levels of implied volatility.

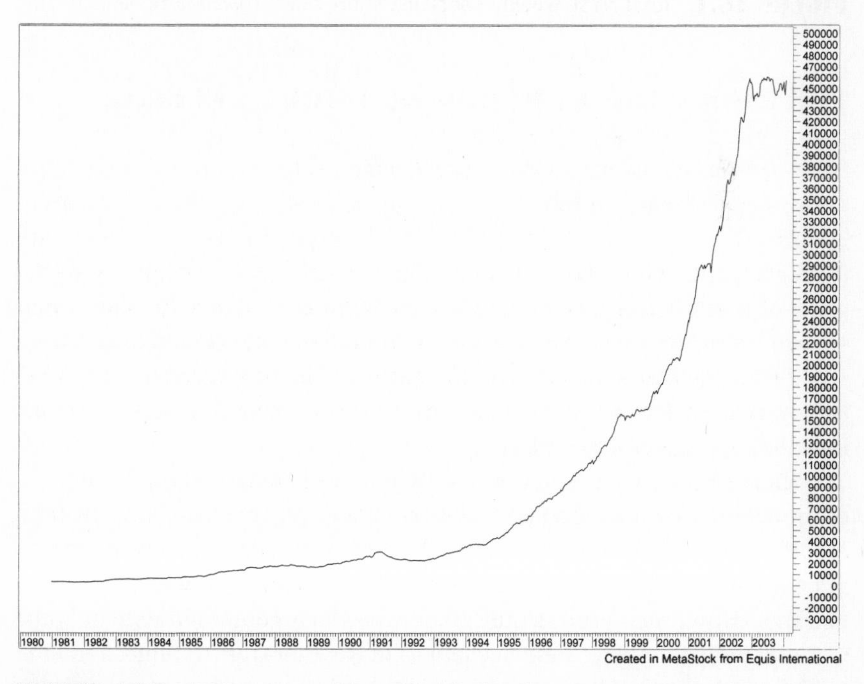

FIGURE 16.2 NYSE total weekly public short sales. (*Data Source:* Pinnacle Data.)

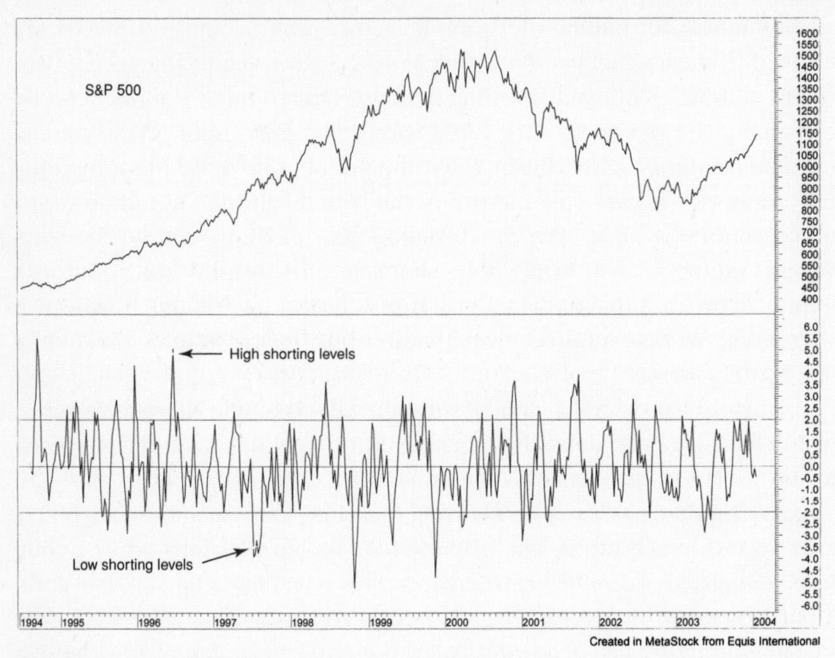

FIGURE 16.3 Public short sales detrended and normalized (using total NYSE volume). (*Data Source:* Pinnacle Data.)

THE RISKS AND REWARDS OF SHORT SELLING

Short-selling activity in stocks is often deemed extremely risky and difficult to do, something better left to the trading professionals. The stock market historically exhibits a long-term bullish directional bias. Combined with the fact that there is theoretically unlimited risk in shorting because the price of a stock has no price limits on the upside, it would appear that shorting is riskier than buying stocks. One added dimension to using intensified short-selling activity as an indicator is that, if wrong, traders need to buy back their open short positions, thus providing a catalyst for gains in stocks and the stock market.

Short sellers, who face potentially unlimited losses should the price of the security continue to move higher, can thus get trigger-happy. In commodity markets the same logic applies, except that historically, prices do not exhibit the same secular tendencies to move higher, as they do in stock markets. However, there is still great risk since commodities can spike higher rapidly following sudden changes in weather (for example, a frost in coffee regions) driving prices up and catching short traders by surprise. It is this potential for unlimited losses that forces short sellers to "cover" or buy back their stock positions in a hurry as they are "squeezed," often alluded to in the business media as "short covering rallies."

What is interesting about short-selling activity, however, is that many of this selling tends to intensify as the stock market begins to trend lower, or the price of a stock declines over a period of time. The greater the decline, the greater the short selling sales, and the greater pressure on the price—the reverse of the cycle outlined above. Of course, if short interest is increasing, it ultimately represents potential purchasing power, as mentioned above, since shorts eventually need to cover-buy their positions. Therefore, it represents an excellent gauge of sentiment, particularly because short selling also tells us that there is potential fuel for sustained upside moves if the shorting activity is at extremes. And it provides substantial potential momentum for rallies if a trader goes against this crowd at the correct time.

Based on the above, is it any surprise that indicators built on short-selling activity have remained popular contrary opinion trading tools? Despite changes in financial markets that have altered the usefulness of certain types of short sales data, the basic idea still has merit. Below I will discuss the history of the indicator and short sales data and what works best today. In the following chapter I built a trading system from this data.

THE HISTORY OF THE INDICATOR

The history of short-selling indicators begins with the odd-lot short-selling ratio. It was based on the idea that odd lots (trade orders or lots of less than 100 shares) were thought to represent the unprofessional small investor or trader with little market sophistication, someone who makes incorrect emotional decisions at market extremes. Remember, the theory of contrary opinion states that the market is most predictable when participants are generally of one mind about its likely direction. The view is generally reinforced by the media, which ultimately draws in all available longs or shorts by its repeated reporting of the prevailing trend. The last entrants, of course, tend to be the least sophisticated among the crowd. In regards to odd-lot short sales, therefore, too much of this activity means the market is ready to stop declining. This "greater fool" mechanism eventually comes to an end, as the last ones short sorely learn.

Investor sentiment gauges that can identify these relatively uninformed traders and investors, therefore, may perform well, which was precisely the logic behind the now antiquated odd-lot short-selling ratio (OLSR).

THE DEMISE OF THE ODD-LOT SHORT SALES RATIO

After a successful period, the OLSR lost its usefulness. The OLSR suffered its demise from the arrival of listed put options in the late 1970s, a development I return to shortly. The OLSR, which measured the activity of the perennial losers on Wall Street, was constructed as a normalized value, usually taking the daily average of overall odd-lot purchases and sales as the denominator in the ratio, and total daily odd-lot short sales as the numerator.

This construction, therefore, captured the intensity of short selling relative to overall odd-lot activity, rather than overall shorting activity in the market as a whole, a construction I employ in Chapter 17 using a more useful short sales data series. Low levels of the ratio (little interest in short selling by odd-lotters) indicated that the small and unprofessional trader or investor believed prices were going to rise; as a result, prices would fall. High levels of the ratio (indicating odd-lot short-selling intensity) revealed that the dumb money was betting on a market decline and prices would rise instead. For more than three decades, this powerful measure actually worked quite well.

As mentioned above, the rise of listed put options brought about the demise of the odd-lot short sale ratio. The purchase of put options, with known and limited risk, became the new way for the crowd to place bets on expected or in-motion market declines. They are well suited to the small, unprofessional trader because no margin deposits are required. In addition, short- or long-term options could be purchased depending on the time horizon of the trader. We have already seen how put volume, when measured against total call option volume (or even total option volume in the case of bond futures), can produce very good market timing signals. Put/call ratios, I would argue, are driven today by the same crowd psychology behind the old odd-lot ratio. In effect, it is the old odd-lot crowd masquerading in new clothes—but still as dependable as ever at getting it wrong.

ODD-LOTTERS AS SMART MONEY?

More recent behavior suggests the odd-lot ratio may behave better as a smart money indicator; this is due to today's heavy use of odd-lots by specialists and other larger traders who are trading in odd-lots to circumvent the NYSE up-tick rule. While I do not delve into that question in this book, it might be worth the effort. The odd-lot ratio, like the OEX put/call ratio (as I showed in Chapter 6), today works better as a measure of correct market sentiment, not the wrong sentiment of the crowd.

In order to understand why this might be the case, you first need to understand how the data is collected and organized. Since short selling is considered a legitimate trading activity with its own associated risks, there are regulations of this activity. The most well known is the prohibition on short selling when the best bid price is on a down-tick, or lower than the previous inside best bid on any stock, generally referred to as the NYSE "up-tick rule."

The NYSE up-tick rule, however, has a loophole. If you are an odd-lotter (trading in lots less than 100), you can skirt the rule. For example, a specialist or member of the NYSE could sell on a down-tick if the size is 99 shares or less. Therefore, the odd-lot indicators may have become polluted with "smart money" traders, rendering this ineffective as an indicator of the unsophisticated crowd. And with most of the dumb money having moved from odd-lots to put options, especially on the QQQs and other ETFs, the odd-lotter may actually be today's smart money in disguise.

ODD-LOT BALANCE INDEX (OLBX)

Another data series that was useful for traders is the odd-lot balance index (OBLX); it measures the ratio of odd-lot sales relative to purchases, producing a value that would range above and below 1.0. Below 1.0 indicated net buying, and above 1.0 net selling by odd-lotters, who almost invariably got it wrong at market turning points when the OLBX was near relative extremes (high suggested that odd-lotters were getting too bearish and low suggested that they were getting too bullish). These corresponded with extreme readings above and below 1.0 on the OBLX. Typically, this data is smoothed with a moving average method, which helps to remove market "noise" from distorted daily movements of the series.

Sadly, this indicator of the buying and selling activity of the smallest traders also lost its predictive power during the mid-1960s with the evolution of financial markets, again partly as a result of the growth of options trading.

OTHER SHORT-SELLING DATA AND RATIOS

One of the most widely quoted shorting activity indicators is the monthly NYSE short interest ratio. While not too useful for our purposes, it is a good conceptual starting point. It enables us to better understand the underlying shorting activity and how to best use the data. NASD firms are mandated to provide the NYSE with all short positions on the 15th of each month. If the 15th is not a business day, the deadline date defaults to the previous business day. The monthly report presents total short interest and the short interest ratio for both the NYSE and NASDAQ exchanges. This report includes short interest and short interest ratios for individual stocks as well.

The short interest data is defined as all open short positions as of the deadline date, usually the 15th. This is to be distinguished from short sales, which I discuss below, because this open interest represents all short sales that have *not been offset*, and thus remain open as of the deadline. The short interest ratio, meanwhile, is simply the total short interest at the end of each monthly period divided by the NYSE average daily trading volume. The ratio provides a relative measure of shorting, relative to how active the Big Board trading has been.

The monthly NYSE absolute levels of short interest, however, are distorted by merger arbitrage, particularly in bull markets when this activity is running high. The short interest ratio also lumps together public and member trading activity, so we are left without a measure of the less sophisticated crowd. For these reasons they are not very useful gauges to use in trading systems.

THE NYSE WEEKLY MEMBERS REPORT

In Table 16.1, the NYSE weekly members report data is presented. This data, which is delayed for two weeks before release to the public, is the basis for

TABLE 16.1 NYSE Members Report for the Week of July 11, 2003

Total Volume	**Week 7/11/03**	**Previous Week**	**Year-Ago Week**
Weekly Total Volume	7,297,186	5,591,373	8,105,731
Daily Average Volume	1,459,437	1,397,843	1,621,146
Short Sales	941,621	733,181	973,584
Public	462,189	372,045	475,094
Member	479,432	361,136	498,490
Specialist	304,372	238,879	366,762
Floor Traders	240	200	1,133
Other Members	174,820	122,057	130,595
Specialist/Public %	.7	.6	.8
Member/Public %	1.0	1.0	1.0

several short sales ratios that I use in my trading systems. I construct my favorite shorting activity indicator from this data, which is then programmed into a trading system. As you can see, short sales are parsed into several categories of traders. Most of the volume is concentrated in three groups: public, specialist, and member. These three groups, and their shorting activity, provide valuable data about what the smart traders and the unsophisticated traders are thinking, the latter being the group that I am looking to track. Taking a look at the public short sales category in Table 16.1, you can see that for the week of July 11, 2003, public short sales totaled 462,189 shares. The public short sales ratio can be created by dividing this number by total short sales activity for the week (941,621). For this week, the public short sales ratio was .49 (462,189/941.621 = .49). Figure 16.4 provides a look at recent movements of this ratio.

While some sentiment technicians still use the ratio of short sales by the public to short sales by specialists (public–specialist short sales ratio), this does not seem to produce a reliable indicator any more. Nevertheless, the idea is that if the public is going short relative to the specialist, or smart

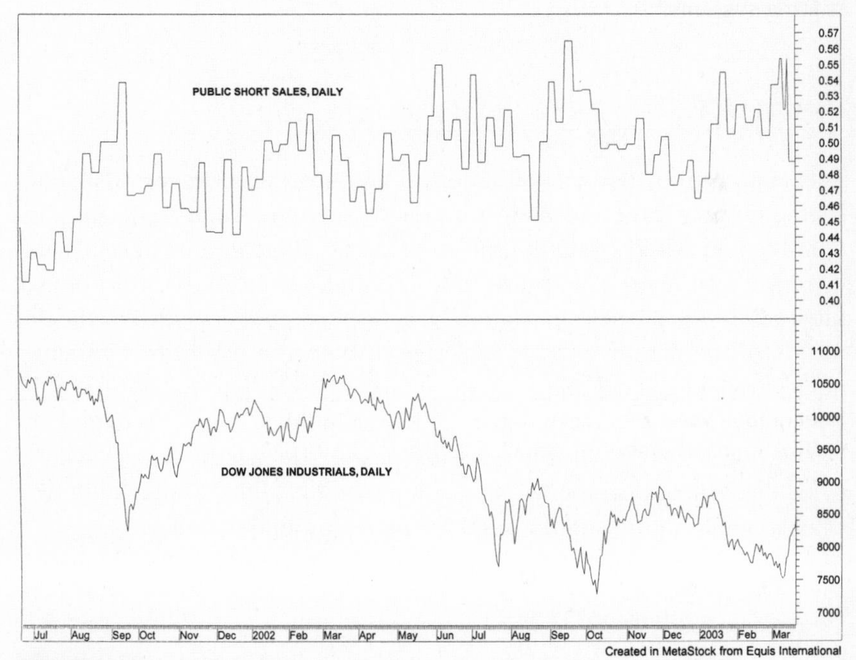

FIGURE 16.4 NYSE public short sales ratio and Dow Jones average.
(*Data Source:* Pinnacle Data.)

money, then they are likely to be wrong about the market's direction (the assumption is that the smart money must be better informed), especially at extreme readings of this indicator. However, this indicator suffers from a number of problems, such as distortion by merger arbitrage activity similar to the monthly report, which can become quite large during bull markets.

I can briefly explain why this distortion occurs. Merger arbitrage distorts the overall levels of short sales because when arbitrageurs speculate on an announced merger, they typically will buy the target company. This tends to trade at a discount to the announced purchase price due to the risk of the merger not happening, and then the arbitrageurs short the acquiring company. The spread between the two should narrow as the completion date approaches and begins to appear a done deal, thus the target company stock rises, narrowing the spread (which can produce an arbitrage profit). So how does this affect our indicators? The short sales of the acquiring company get counted in the weekly and monthly numbers released by the NYSE. This can be quite heavy in bull markets, especially near tops when the mood gets frothy and there are many merger deals announced. Yet this activity is clearly not directional speculation, and is in fact a market-neutral trading strategy. The result is that it artificially increases the recorded level of total short-selling activity.

SUMMARY

This chapter provides a brief historical and analytical overview of short-selling activity data and indicators used by sentiment technicians. The monthly and weekly data is used to calculate short interest levels, short interest ratios, short sales ratios, and the odd-lot short sales ratio. Some of the weaknesses of these indicators have been pointed out, such as the distortion of the data by merger arbitrage activity, the rise of odd-lot smart money traders, the migration of old odd-lotters to options markets, and the long delay in the release of data. The weekly public short sales data, however, is one series that remains very useful, even though this data is delayed by two weeks. In Chapter 17, I test a short-selling trading system built with weekly public short sales data and run on major market indices.

CHAPTER 17

Public Shorts: Still as Good as Ever as Crowd "Sentimeter"

To improve the use of short-selling data, some sentiment technicians prefer to use the public-only short-selling activity, also known as the nonmember short sales ratio. Like our options buyers, these public short sellers do not have a very good reputation for predicting market moves, and are thus excellent indicators for trading against the crowd. The public shorts are almost invariably wrong about the market direction, especially when absolute levels of participation (overall short selling) is running high. As with put buying, too much pessimism (increased short sales) generally signals that a market bottom is near. Conversely, too much optimism (decreased short sales) historically has marked the end of a bull market, or bullish market trend.

With these issues in mind, I construct a trading system in this chapter using a normalized public short sales ratio (NPSR) that is available weekly. There are two data streams required to construct the series; the weekly short sales by the public and the total weekly short sales volume. There are other ways to manipulate the data, such as normalizing with NYSE total trading volume (used in the oscillator chart in the previous chapter), but I do not venture down that road with testing in this chapter. To remove unwanted trends in the data, NPSR is processed in one of my oscillators using the difference between four- and eight-week exponential moving averages.

NORMALIZED WEEKLY PUBLIC SHORT SALES TRADING SYSTEM TEST

The system I use in this chapter is proprietary, but runs on the data outlined above. NSPR produces excellent results despite its two week public release delay.

The contrarian logic behind this system is as follows: When the NPSR oscillator has gotten too high, the assumption is that there has been too much shorting activity with presumably more open interest, thus a potential rally exists. When the oscillator value has been too low, the assumption is that there has been too little shorting activity (and presumably less short open interest) and a potential market decline awaits. By applying the correct triggers to actually get into trades, it might be possible to catch some of the short and long squeezes that occur on the heels of too little or too much shorting activity by the public.

The results of data testing are presented in Tables 17.1 through 17.4 for the Dow Jones Industrial Average (DJIA), S&P 500 stock index, NASDAQ 100,

TABLE 17.1 NPSR Proprietary System Test on DJIA. No Stops Were Used. (Points Test.)

Total net profit	15,046.97	Largest win	1,572.3
Buy/Hold profit	6849.8	Largest loss	−522.65
Days in test	3668	Average length of win	7.83
Total closed trades	64	Average length of loss	2.93
Commissions paid	0.00	Longest winning trade	32
Average profit per trade	220.6	Longest losing trade	9
Average Win/Average Loss ratio	3.63	Most consecutive wins	4
		Most consecutive losses	3
Total long trades	32	Total bars out	142
Total short trades	32	Average length out	7.47
Winning long trades	21	Longest out period	13
Winning short trades	14	System close drawdown	0.00
Total winning trades	35	Profit/Loss index	78.29
Total losing trades	29	System open drawdown	0.00
Amount of winning trades	18,293.3	Reward/Risk index	100.0
Amount of losing trades	−4,171.98	Maximum open trade drawdown	−811.6
Average win	522.7		
Average loss	−143.86	Buy/Hold index	133.18

TABLE 17.2 NPSR Proprietary System Test on S&P 500. (Points Test.)

Total net profit	1,605.85	Largest win	294.87
Buy/Hold profit	697.05	Largest loss	–63.08
Days in test	3493	Average length of win	8.67
Total closed trades	61	Average length of loss	3.03
Commissions paid	0.00	Longest winning trade	52
Average profit per trade	24.9	Longest losing trade	8
Average Win/ Average Loss ratio	3.70	Most consecutive wins	4
		Most consecutive losses	4
Total long trades	32	Total bars out	120
Total short trades	29	Average length out	7.5
Winning long trades	17	Longest out period	18
Winning short trades	13	System close drawdown	–7.71
Total winning trades	30	Profit/Loss index	73.15
Total losing trades	31	System open drawdown	–19.54
Amount of winning trades	2,108.8	Reward/Risk index	98.8
Amount of losing trades	589.6	Maximum open trade drawdown	–159.79
Average win	70.3		
Average loss	–63	Buy/Hold index	142.8

TABLE 17.3 NASDAQ 100/NPSR Proprietary Trading System. (Points Test)

Total net profit	4388.29	Largest win	1,067.7
Buy/Hold profit	1,163.22	Largest loss	–435.34
Days in test	3668	Average length of win	7.28
Total closed trades	68	Average length of loss	3.00
Commissions paid	0.00	Longest winning trade	26
Average profit per trade	62.4	Longest losing trade	9
Average Win/Average Loss ratio	2.93	Most consecutive wins	4
		Most consecutive losses	3
Total long trades	36	Total bars out	148
Total short trades	32	Average length out	6.73
Winning long trades	21	Longest out period	17
Winning short trades	15	System close drawdown	–3.00
Total winning trades	36	Profit/Loss index	70.39
Total losing trades	32	System open drawdown	–6.02
Amount of winning trades	15272.07	Reward/Risk index	99.86
Amount of losing trades	–6,088.08	Maximum open trade drawdown	–1099.13
Average win	169.1		
Average loss	–57.69	Buy/Hold index	289.85

TABLE 17.4 RUSSELL 2000/NPSR Proprietary Trading System. (Points Test)

Total net profit	876.35	Largest win	84.02
Buy/Hold profit	290.15	Largest loss	–62.02
Days in test	3080	Average length of win	7.13
Total closed trades	61	Average length of loss	2.10
Commissions paid	0.00	Longest winning trade	16
Average profit per trade	13.36	Longest losing trade	5
Average Win/Average		Most consecutive wins	3
Loss ratio	4.75	Most consecutive losses	3
Total long trades	31	Total bars out	142
Total short trades	30	Average length out	7.47
Winning long trades	20	Longest out period	14
Winning short trades	10	System close drawdown	0.00
Total winning trades	30	Profit/Loss index	79.45
Total losing trades	31	System open drawdown	–1.67
Amount of winning trades	1041.76	Reward/Risk index	99.81
Amount of losing trades	–226.67	Maximum open	
Average win	34.72	trade drawdown	–51.86
Average loss	–7.31	Buy/Hold index	223.15

and Russell 2000. The dates in this sample period are July 1, 1994 through January 22, 2004.

Starting with total net profits, the DJIA test produced a spectacular 15,046.97 points with a buy/hold level of 6,849.8; however, there was a dizzying maximum open trade drawdown of –811.6 points even though the system close drawdown was zero. All the vital statistics were quite good otherwise, with a 100.00 reward/risk index. Looking at the S&P 500, meanwhile, results were equally good, with 1,605.85 points extracted from the period studied compared with a buy/hold profit of 697.05 points (see Table 17.2). There was a –159.79 point open trade swoon in the system, but otherwise the vital stats are stellar. They include an average-win-to-average-loss ratio of 3.70! Total number of trades was 61 with 30 winners. The largest loss was –63.08, which is not too bad given the absolute level of net profit. Looking at Figure 17.1, the equity plot reveals some flat zones, but otherwise the growth is quite stable and certainly viable.

The two other markets also did very well. The NASDAQ 100 and Russell 2000 test runs pulled out 4,388.29 and 876.35 points, respectively. The NASDAQ 100 maximum open trade drawdown was –1,099.13 points, which would be hard to stomach for most traders; however, in the context of absolute returns and consistency of performance across this long test period, it cannot be denied that this system holds great prom-

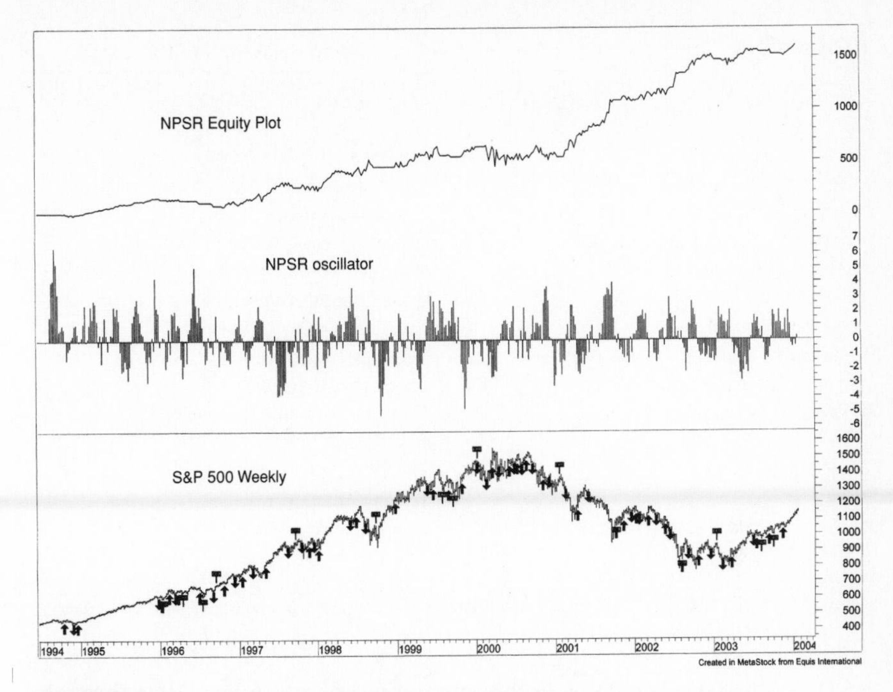

FIGURE 17.1 Equity plot for NPSR test on S&P 500. (*Source:* Maridome International.)

ise. Other vital statistics were well within acceptable parameters, as seen in Table 17.3 and Table 17.4. By applying this system simultaneously to these markets as a group, much of the equity swings can be smoothed, although certainly not eliminated altogether.

SUMMARY

Public short-selling volume derived from the NYSE weekly members report was used as a normalized ratio and detrended with differencing using slow- and fast-moving averages similar to the previous systems. The proprietary system tests performed on four major stock market indices produced total net profits that surpass all other system performance. While large swings in open trades were apparent, the very large absolute levels of net gains suggest that this approach offers great potential if applied with the correct money management methods.

CHAPTER 18

Trading Against the Advisory Opinion Crowd

First applied systematically by Abraham Cohen, tabulating and quantifying the advice of the market experts is still used by sentiment technicians today for medium- and long-term timing of the stock market. The basic idea is similar to the other approaches I have examined. In this case, though, it is the opinion of market "experts" that is wrong, even though they are the supposed professionals.

Too much optimism by advisors, for example, means there are likely to be few potential buyers left—assuming investors are following their advice, of course. Conversely, too much pessimism by the advisors suggests that there might not be many sellers left, creating potential for many buyers (and short covering power rallies). Extreme levels, like with other indicators I have examined, generally produce the best signals.

ADVISORY OPINION DATA SOURCES

Cohen's percentage of bullish and bearish advisors is still available from *Investors Intelligence*. In addition to *Investors Intelligence* data, this chapter uses the opinion of market advisors from another excellent source, *Bullish Consensus*. Started by Earl Hadady, *Bullish Consensus* numbers are published by Market Vane today. Collected from advisory services and newsletters for the futures and commodity markets, *Bullish Consensus* numbers are constructed and normalized as an index number between 0 and 100. If the *Bullish Consensus* number is high, there are more bullish advisors; if the number is low, there are fewer bullish advisors.

This service is provided both on a daily and weekly basis. It is compiled from buy and sell recommendations of top market advisors from over

30 futures markets, including the stock market. Data is collected from market advisor newsletters, well-known brokerage houses, and phone, fax, and e-mail recommendations.

The *Bullish Consensus* numbers measure the intensity of bullish sentiment (but not necessarily actual positions). For example, a low reading of 17 for S&P 500 futures would indicate that there are very few bullish advisors. In other words, just 17 percent of the advisors have bullish outlooks, which means that the market is oversold, and that a reversal is possibly nearby.

First tabulated in 1964 as a way to determine when to take positions against the crowd in futures markets, the idea is that a market eventually exhausts all the buyers in bullish moves, or all the sellers during extended bearish declines, so traders can position for a reaction, opposite the prevailing thinking of this crowd.

Another excellent source of data about investor sentiment that is tested in this chapter is the American Association of Independent Investors (AAII) survey of members' medium-term outlook on the stock market (six months ahead). This is an excellent source of investor sentiment that tracks bullish and bearish sentiment, like *Investors Intelligence*, but with one important difference; it directly samples investors, not their advisors.

Finally, I have developed my own public opinion gauge, which I present in the final chapter of this book. It represents, as far as I know, the only attempt to systematically quantify the intensity of bearish and bullish news flow. In addition, I test this investor sentiment data on the broad market.

TESTING "EXPERT" AND INDIVIDUAL INVESTOR OPINION

The setups used on newsletter opinion data are similar to that used in the previous chapters on put/call ratios data. The first test applied is a version of Squeeze Play II. I run the system separately on each of the three sources of opinion mentioned above: *Investors Intelligence*, *Bullish Consensus*, and the American Association of Individual Investors.

The trading rules for this version of Squeeze Play II are presented in Table 18.1. This is a weekly data series so the oscillator is constructed with a one-week value differenced with a four-week (EMA1-4W). Price triggers or not, these systems make a nice profit as shown in Table 18.2 and 18.3 on each of the sources of opinion outlined above. The dates covered in the test run from January 3, 1997 through January 22, 2004.

TABLE 18.1 EMA1-4W Squeeze Play II Rules for Advisory Opinion Data—Entries/Exits

EMA1-4W Squeeze Play II Rules—Entries	
Enter long position when EMA1-4W highest high value is greater than 5 percent *and* this week's close is *greater* than last week's high.	Enter short position when the EMA1-4W lowest low value is less than –5 percent *and* this week's close is *less* than last week's low.
EMA1-4 Squeeze Play II Rules—Exits	
Exit long position when the EMA1-4W lowest low value is less than zero *and* this week's close is *less* than last week's low.	Exit short position when the EMA1-4W highest high value is greater than zero *and* this week's close is *greater* than last week's high.

TABLE 18.2 EMA1-4W Squeeze Play II Test—S&P 500 (Investors Intelligence)

Total net profit	489.08	Largest win	154.02
Buy/Hold profit	383.04	Largest loss	–153.79
Days in test	2,576	Average length of win	12.5
Total closed trades	20	Average length of loss	7.88
Commissions paid	0.00	Longest winning trade	21
Average profit per trade	21.90	Longest losing trade	34
Average Win/Average		Most consecutive wins	7
Loss ratio	1.71	Most consecutive losses	3
Total long trades	11	Total bars out	181
		Average length out	18.10
Total short trades	9	Longest out period	32
		System close drawdown	–141.44
Winning long trades	8	Profit/Loss index	63.71
Winning short trades	4		
Total winning trades	12	System open drawdown	–230.64
Total losing trades	8	Reward/Risk index	67.95
Amount of winning trades	716.48	Maximum open	
		trade drawdown	–138.84
Amount of losing trades	–278.57	Buy/Hold index	41.04
Average win	59.71		
Average loss	–34.82		

TABLE 18.3 Market Vane EMA1-4W Squeeze Play II Test—S&P 500

Total net profit	662.25	Largest win	226.38
Buy/Hold profit	383.04	Largest loss	−144.27
Days in test	2,576	Average length of win	14.07
Total closed trades	27	Average length of loss	10.00
Commissions paid	0.00	Longest winning trade	30
Average profit per trade	19.34	Longest losing trade	48
Average Win/Average Loss ratio	1.35	Most consecutive wins	4
		Most consecutive losses	3
Total long trades	13	Total bars out	43
		Average length out	43.00
Total short trades	14	Longest out period	43
		System close drawdown	−50.28
Winning long trades	8		
Winning short trades	7	Profit/Loss index	46.61
Total winning trades	15		
Total losing trades	12	System open drawdown	−97.63
Amount of winning trades	1280.60	Reward/Risk index	87.15
Amount of losing trades	−758.44	Maximum open trade drawdown	−212.58
Average win	85.37		
Average loss	−63.20	Buy/Hold index	109.47

The same system, run on AAII's bearish opinion index, meanwhile, also produced a profit, but the total net profit of 251 index points did not beat the buy-and-hold number of 383 for the period. Table 18.3 presents the run on Market Vane's *Bullish Consensus* data for the S&P 500, which has to reverse the rules because it measures bullish—not bearish—opinion. It produced excellent results with 662 index points captured compared with the buy/hold amount of 383. System close drawdown was −50, which is larger than most of tests done in previous chapters, but still acceptable given the overall performance. Trading this system with an S&P 500 futures contract and an initial account size of $30,000 would have produced an annualized rate of return of 79 percent.

Another way to test this data is to create a ratio of the bull-and-bear indices, which is something I do with news flow in the next chapter. There are two tests I conduct with this approach, one on the *Investors Intelligence* bull/bear ratio and one on AAII's bull/bear ratio. The AAII tests produced

171 points in total net profit, still below the buy/hold approach. The *Investors Intelligence* bull/bear ratio did slightly better with 262 points, but still not good enough. This limited number of tests, therefore, seems to point to bear opinion as having more predictive power than bull opinion guages.

SUMMARY

Further tests should be carried out with different oscillator speeds and possibly different trading setups on this important data. Optimization routines might be run on threshold levels to evaluate different sentiment levels for setting up the trades. Nevertheless, the crowd again has shown itself to be a good predictor of market turns, with bearish opinion data from *Investors Intelligence*, AAII, and Market Vane's *Bullish Consensus* showing the best results. While I did not obtain overall results superior to other data tested in this book, this may be due to the fact that this is opinion and not necessarily what investors are doing. Yet there is still great potential here for anyone ambitious enough to dig deeper into this data to find some additional trading clues about crowd psychology.

CHAPTER 19

The Fourth Estate Crowd

In his excellent book on stock market pricing behavior entitled, *Irrational Exuberance*, Robert Shiller writes "Nothing beats the stock market for sheer frequency of potentially interesting news items." In this chapter, I measure the intensity of this news flow, the sentiment of the so-called Fourth Estate, in the form of quantitative bull and bear news intensity indices, which I have built from news scans. I then test the data series in a trading system run on equity market indices.

There is no question that news coverage of the stock market helps sell newspapers and get the attention of television and radio viewers, as Shiller implies. But news also tends to foster what Robert Shiller terms an "attention cascade" among investors, leading them to behave in a herd-like manner, which can lead to common misjudgments. If this is true, then a quantification of bearish and bullish news flow might provide another profitable technique to gauge crowd psychology, much like put/call volume ratios, option volatility, short sales, and newsletter opinion.

When stock market price movements prompt editorial desks at the nation's leading newspapers and magazines to increase the frequency and visibility (more headlines and copy) of either bearish or bullish news flow, investors may overreact. Reading a top-of-the-fold article blaring "Panic Selling on Wall Street Sends Stocks Diving," sure can get the attention of investors; they may discuss the bad news at work or home, further cascading the news flow.

For many years, sentiment technicians have used books, magazines, and newspaper cover stories as indications of extreme crowd psychology. Contrarians looked to major cover stories or sensational books about a market as a sign of extreme sentiment; they traded opposite to this news or these publications and thus against the crowd.

It is possible to trade a quantitative news flow series instead, as my database proves. My bull and bear news flow intensity indices can be used much like other data in this book and interpreted in a similar manner: When the level of bullish news flow reaches an extreme, the market is near a top, and when there is a dearth of optimistic news flow and high level of pessimism in the news, the market is headed towards a bottom.

As far as I know, there is no published series like this that captures and quantifies news flow. Aside from some old academic studies that looked at bullish or bearish content of news stories to determine market sentiment extremes and subsequent price behavior, there is no continuous series of objective data that quantifies on a weekly basis (much like put and call volume or investment advisor surveys do) the level of bullishness or bearishness on Wall Street and Main Street.

The advances of computerization and digitized media have enabled the systematic construction of an objective, bull-and-bear news intensity database, which can be updated weekly. Table 19.1 below presents a list of some of the base terms and key words used to construct my proprietary news flow database.

Typically, following a series of rallies, or prolonged bull trend, bullish news flow intensity increases in the media. This increased intensity and frequency of bullish news creates a positive feedback loop. More bullish news flow begets more buyers who feel they are missing out; this sustains the rally as more buyers join in and additional bullish news flow results as markets move even higher. A similar dynamic works for bearish news flow and bearish crowd behavior, perhaps even more powerfully due to the fear factor.

TABLE 19.1 Bull and Bear News Flow Intensity Base Terms and Key Words

Base Terms	Bull News Key Words	Bear News Key Words
Wall Street	Optimism	Pessimism
Investors	Hopes	Worries
Stocks	Soar,	Plunge
Equities	Positive	Negative
Analysts	Upbeat	Panic
Traders	Bullish	Bearish

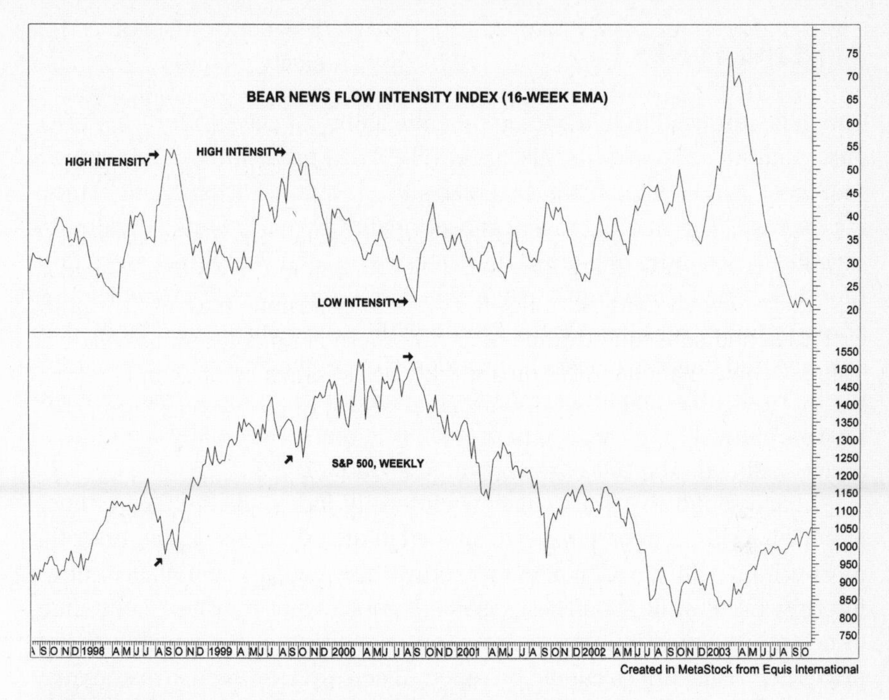

FIGURE 19.1 16-week exponential moving average of bear news intensity index. (*Source:* Summa Capital Management & Research, LLC.)

A look at my bear news intensity series, which has been smoothed with a sixteen-week exponential moving average, shows how news sentiment extremes work like measures of investor sentiment seen elsewhere in this book. In fact, the chart in Figure 19.1 shows that this alternative indicator of crowd sentiment gave excellent warnings of impending major market reversals, most notably the market top of March 2000 and the market bottom of March 2003. The low level of the indicator demonstrates lack of bearish news flow and vice versa. Too much bearish news flow usually signals a market bottom. Note, however, that there is always some news flow that is either bearish or bullish, but when the news flow reaches an extreme, it can signal that a market reversal is nearby.

SYSTEM TESTS

The indicator used in this book to test the ability of news to forecast price movements is a weekly oscillator (BNI4-8EMA) created by differencing a four-week exponential moving average and an eight-week exponential moving average. The raw data used is a normalized weekly series created by dividing the quantity of bearish news stories by total Wall Street news flow (another series I maintain). When this oscillator moves 5 percent either above or below zero (zero is the average), the sentiment is considered at an extreme and thus the market is considered oversold or overbought respectively. To test this hypothesis, I set up some simple trading rules that are nearly identical to those used in previous chapters, essentially a version of Squeeze Play II. The rules are presented in Table 19.2

I have found that the bear news intensity index (BNI4-8EMA), much like the bearish opinion indices examined in the previous chapter, offer the most valuable information about the crowd's behavior. The bull/bear news intensity ratio, while satisfactory, is not as good, which may have something to do with the reaction time of investors to news flow. Presumably, falling prices and rising prices should be reported equally. However, investors may

TABLE 19.2 Bear News Intensity Index (BNI4-8EMA) Trading Rules

Enter long position when the BNI4-8EMA oscillator has been *greater* than 5 percent in the past two weeks and today's high is *greater* than last week's high.	Enter short position when the BNI4-8EMA oscillator has been *less* than 5 percent in the past two weeks and today's low is *less* than the last week's low.
Exit long position *one* week after entry.	Exit short position *one* week after entry.
Exit long position *two* weeks after entry.	Exit short position *two* weeks after entry.
Exit long position *three* weeks after entry.	Exit short position *three* weeks after entry.
Exit long position *four* weeks after entry.	Exit short position *four* weeks after entry.

TABLE 19.3 Bear News Intensity Index Trading System Test (S&P 500)—Longs Only/Exit Week One

Total net profit	82.27	Largest win	114.55
Buy/Hold profit	313.97	Largest loss	-103.61
Days in test	2516	Average length of win	3.00
Total closed trades	35	Average length of loss	3.00
Commissions paid	0.00	Longest winning trade	3
Average profit per trade	2.35	Longest losing trade	3
Average Win/Average Loss ratio	1.09	Most consecutive wins	6
		Most consecutive losses	5
Total long trades	35	Total bars out	327
Total short trades	0	Average length out	9.08
Winning long trades	18	Longest out period	26
Winning short trades	0	System close drawdown	-86.37
Total losing trades	17	Profit/Loss index	13.48
Amount of winning trades	610.33	Total winning trades	18
Maximum open losing trades	-528.06	System open drawdown	-86.37
		Reward/Risk index	48.78
Average win	33.91	Amount of trade drawdown	-88.61
Average loss	-31.06	Buy/Hold index	-73.8

become more irrational and herd-like during market declines than during market rallies, as they can easily panic in big market swoons. Fear may thus be more powerful than greed as an emotional variable to use when trading against the crowd. Table 19.3 contains the results of the first test that incorporates an exit-on-close *one week* following entry into a long trade.

All tests of my news flow indicator are for the period January 3, 1997 through December 26, 2003. With only 82 points in net profit, as seen in Table 19.3, which is below the buy/hold level of 314, and with other vital performance statistics unacceptable, this will not do. However, if we delay the exit for another week, as seen in Table 19.4, performance jumps to 586 index points for longs only (easily beating the buy/hold level), with total winners ahead of losers and a reward/risk index of 100! The average-win-to-average-loss ratio was also an excellent 2.45, with an average profit per trade of 18 points. Clearly, trading off excessive bear news flow has some potential.

TABLE 19.4 Bear News Intensity Index Trading System Test (S&P 500)—Longs Only/Exit Week Two

Total net profit	586.09	Largest win	125.85
Buy/Hold profit	313.97	Largest loss	-71.87
Days in test	2516	Average length of win	4.00
Total closed trades	32	Average length of loss	4.00
Commissions paid	0.00	Longest winning trade	4
Average profit per trade	18.31	Longest losing trade	4
Average Win/Average Loss ratio	2.45	Most consecutive wins	4
		Most consecutive losses	4
Total long trades	32	Total bars out	298
Total short trades	0	Average length out	9.03
Winning long trades	17	Longest out period	24
Winning short trades	0	System close drawdown	0.00
Total winning trades	17	Profit/Loss index	63.99
Total losing trades	15	System open drawdown	0.00
Amount of winning trades	915.98	Reward/Risk index	100.00
Amount of losing trades	-329.89	Maximum open trade drawdown	-88.61
Average win	53.88		
Average loss	-21.99	Buy/Hold index	86.67

The exit plans for weeks three and four also produced excellent total net profits (641 and 659, respectively), with equally good performance profiles. As you can see in Figure 19.2, the BNI4-8EMA oscillator reflects sentiment extremes quite well.

Can shorting the Fourth Estate produce equally good results? That is, when the bearish news flow reaches a low level, does this indicate that investors have been fed too much bullish news and that the stock market is ready for reversal lower? Tables 19.5 and 19.6 indicate that the lack of bullish news flow may be an even better timing indicator. While the week-one exit plan only marginally beat buy/hold profits (yet still a much better performance than the longs-only tests assuming an exit at the end of week one), and week two is essentially flat (–2 points), the third- and fourth-week exit plans produce excellent total net profits: 721 and 491, respectively.

When combining the longs and shorts into one trading system, finally, performance in all the four time frames is positive. However, the third

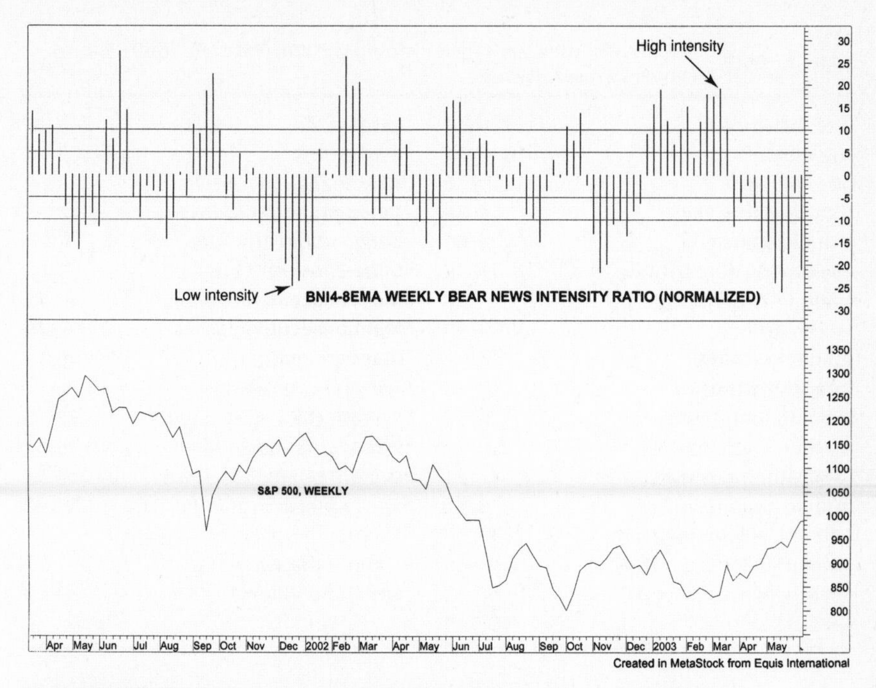

FIGURE 19.2 Bear news intensity BNI4-8EMA oscillator and S&P 500.
(*Source:* Summa Capital Management & Research, LLC.)

week exit strategy is only 4 points, profits having been reduced by the poor performance of the short trades. Tables 19.7 and 19.8 show the best-performing weeks: weeks two and four, with 580 and 943 points of net profit, respectively. Drawdowns, however, are bigger than in previous system tests. Yet, there is a closed system drawdown of zero, and a modest open trade drawdown of just –95 index points in the week four exit plan. Net profit performance for week four beats buy/hold twice over, which is one of the best-performing systems presented in this book. The system rules, it should be pointed out, allow for taking long trades only when not in a short trade and taking short trades only when not in a long trade. There are thus no reversals of open trades.

Finally, Table 19.9 presents a summary of performance of the long/short system using bear news flow. Annualized buy/hold profit for the seven-year

TABLE 19.5 Bear News Intensity Index Trading System Test (S&P 500) Shorts Only/Exit Week Three

Total net profit	720.67	Largest win	219.13
Buy/Hold profit	313.97	Largest loss	−103.15
Days in test	2516	Average length of win	5.00
Total closed trades	39	Average length of loss	5
Commissions paid	0.00	Longest losing trade	5
Average profit per trade	18.48	Most consecutive wins	6
Average Win/Average		Most consecutive losses	5
Loss ratio	1.97	Total bars out	245
Total long trades	0	Average length out	6.13
Total short trades	39	Longest out period	14
Winning long trades	0	System close drawdown	−124.6
Winning short trades	21	Profit/Loss index	56.51
Total winning trades	21	System open drawdown	−132.58
Total losing trades	18	Reward/Risk index	84.46
Amount of winning trades	1275.33	Maximum open	
Amount of losing trades	−554.66	trade drawdown	−63.13
Average win	60.73	Buy/Hold index	129.53
Average loss	−30.814		

TABLE 19.6 Bear News Intensity Index Trading System Test (S&P 500) Shorts Only/Exit Week Four

Total net profit	491.06	Largest win	164.23
Buy/Hold profit	313.97	Largest loss	−106.28
Days in test	2516	Average length of win	6.00
Total closed trades	32	Average length of loss	6.00
Commissions paid	0.00	Longest winning trade	6
Average profit per trade	15.35	Longest losing trade	6
Average Win/Average		Most consecutive wins	6
Loss ratio	1.70	Most consecutive losses	5
Total long trades	0	Total bars out	232
Total short trades	32	Average length out	7.03
Winning long trades	0	Longest out period	13
Winning short trades	17	System close drawdown	−106.16
Total winning trades	17	Profit/Loss index	48.10
Total losing trades	15	System open drawdown	−143.55
Amount of winning trades	1020.93	Reward/Risk index	77.38
Amount of losing trade	−529.87	Maximum open	
Average win	60.05	trade drawdown	−92.72
Average loss	−35.33	Buy/Hold index	70.95

TABLE 19.7 Bear News Intensity Index Trading System (S&P 500) Longs/Shorts Exit Week Two

Total net profit	579.98	Largest win	125.85
Buy/Hold profit	313.97	Largest loss	–79.88
Days in test	2516	Average length of win	4.28
Total closed trades	60	Average length of loss	4.00
Commissions paid	0.00	Longest winning trade	5
Average profit per trade	9.67	Longest losing trade	4
Average Win/Average Loss ratio	1.56	Most consecutive wins	9
		Most consecutive losses	5
Total long trades	25	Total bars out	231
Total short trades	35	Average length out	4.44
Winning long trades	15	Longest out period	15
Winning short trades	17	System close drawdown	0.00
Total winning trades	32	Profit/Loss index	43.95
Total losing trades	28	System open drawdown	0.00
Amount of winning trades	1319.63	Reward/Risk index	100.00
Amount of losing trades	–739.65	Maximum open trade drawdown	–62.99
Average win	41.24		
Average loss	–26.42	Buy/Hold index	101.91

TABLE 19.8 Bear News Intensity Index Trading System Test (S&P 500)—Longs/Shorts Exit Week Four

Total net profit	942.85	Largest win	214.30
Buy/Hold profit	313.97	Largest loss	–108.00
Days in test	2516	Average length of win	6.35
Total closed trades	44	Average length of loss	6.83
Commissions paid	0.00	Longest winning trade	9
Average profit per trade	21.4284	Longest losing trade	9
Average Win/Average Loss ratio	1.67	Most consecutive wins	4
		Most consecutive losses	3
Total long trades	16	Total bars out	174
Total short trades	28	Average length out	4.70
Winning long trades	11	Longest out period	12
Winning short trades	15	System close drawdown	0.00
Total winning trades	26	Profit/Loss index	58.43
Total losing trades	18	System open drawdown	–11.49
Amount of winning trades	1613.58	Reward/Risk index	98.80
Amount of losing trades	–670.73	Maximum open trade drawdown	–95.27
Average win	62.0608		
Average loss	–37.2628	Buy/Hold index	208.95

TABLE 19.9 Performance Summary of Long/Short Using Bear News Flow Profit and Percentage Gain Based on $30,000 Account Value for Each Exit Plan on S&P 500

Exit Time Frames	Net Profit (Points)	Net Profit ($)	Total Return (%)	Average Return/Year (%)
1st week exit	450.08	112,520	375.07	53.58
2nd week exit	579.98	144,995	483.32	69.04
3rd week exit	737.9702	184,492.5	614.98	87.85
4th week exit	942.85	235,712.5	785.71	112.24
Totals	2,710.88	677,720	2,259.08	80.68

period is 37.26 percent (not shown in Table 19.9); this was surpassed in all but the week-three exit plan tests. Average annual return for the group as a whole came in at 80.68 percent, which easily beat the buy/hold rate of 37.26 percent when all the trading periods are accounted for, so there is no cherry picking here.

SUMMARY

It appears from the tests presented in this chapter that, as a group, investors overreact to news. We see this clear pattern in the S&P 500 over periods of one to four weeks, following extreme levels of either low bearish news flow (tops) or high bearish news flow (bottoms). If markets were efficient, news flow that already has been digested should be "stale" and would have no value at predicting future price movements. This claim, however, is called into question with the results presented here. Indeed, it would appear that the theory that markets correctly price all known information efficiently is the illusion, not that prices appear to be too low or too high.

CHAPTER 20

Postscript on Crowd Psychology in Financial Markets

If we are to believe the economic theory of efficient markets, then the profits derived from back testing that are presented in this book are not attainable. The weak version of the efficient markets hypothesis (EMH) states that it is not possible to predict future prices with past, publicly available information. This is an intriguing claim since it relegates all system developers to one of two camps. In one group are those sincere but misdirected traders who do not know that their actions are pure folly. In the other group are those who produce and sell systems they know will ultimately not work. In either case, looking for patterns in price charts or secondary data streams that can be harnessed into trading systems simply is not possible according to the EMH, whether technicians are well intentioned or not.

The second form of the EMH, known as the semi-strong version, allows for some above-normal profits to be made from such trading systems. While a trading system may be effective for a time, though, profits will soon be arbitraged away as trading patterns and methods become widely known and traded by others. It is interesting that this assumes that this knowledge becomes publicly available for traders to exploit. It is entirely possible, for example (and likely), that profitable systems remain proprietary, the private domain of the trader who developed them, and therefore not available for other traders to learn and apply.

After all, many hedge funds and managed futures trading programs operate with undisclosed proprietary systems, which is why they earn high management and incentive fees. There are many such contradictions in the reasoning of EMH theorists, most of whom are academics and not traders.

The strong version of EMH, finally, is widely not considered to hold water. It claims that it is not possible even for those with privileged knowledge to profit. This is obviously contradicted by repeated patterns of illegal insider trading which, if it were not for vigilance on the part of the Securities and Exchange Commission, would probably be a regular source of super profits for those with access to insider knowledge. In fact, there are still plenty of legal differential rates of access to valuable knowledge that exist; they are thus a potential source of insider trading profit for those with the information. Delayed release of short-selling and short-interest data, for example, allows specialists who know how much short selling is taking place to capitalize on it prior to the general public.

REFLECTIONS ON EMH AND THE PSYCHOLOGY OF THE CROWD

The research conducted for this book has in part been done with the claims of EMH adherents in mind. Does the theory of crowd psychology, noticeably absent in a discussion by the EMH faithful, pose a major challenge to the school's claims?

Rereading *A Random Walk Down Wall Street* by Burton G. Malkiel, perhaps one of the most widely read defenses of the EMH, I was surprised to find no mention of contrary opinion theory among his survey of failed trading systems. Perhaps this is due to serious challenges that the theory poses to EMH in all its forms. To begin to understand the severity of the threat, I want to discuss an important point raised by challengers to EMH who are known as behavioral finance theorists. Behavioral finance is a relatively new trend in economic theory that arose largely in response to the growing number of empirical anomalies and theoretical contradictions of EMH.

The semi-strong version of EMH allows for some exceptions to the main claim as encapsulated in the quotation from Robert Shiller found at the beginning of this book. However, it hinges critically on the ability of arbitragers to push prices back in line with fundamentals. But what if the smart money is not capable of pushing prices back to fundamental values, due to either the so-called smart money not having the risk tolerance or interest to go against the crowd, nor the capital to move markets in the other direction?

In fact, many professional money managers (not traditionally considered members of the unsophisticated crowd), due to competitive pressures to perform, might find it—at least in the short run—more advantageous to *follow* the crowd and the accompanying price momentum. This can be a reinforcing, circular dynamic, leading to large price distortions.

This behavior was seen in the extended rally in the late 1990s. Why fight such a powerful trend, especially when it can produce quick profits? If the mutual fund crowd thinks alike in this manner, and since they are arguably the primary market movers in today's markets, it is hard to imagine how the semi-strong version of EMH can hold, that markets are kept efficient by smart money.

Indeed, as the cycles of investor sentiment quantified and tested in this book appear to indicate, something other than efficient markets created by an assumed all-knowing investor exists. I argue that markets are largely driven by fluid cycles of investor sentiment (professional and nonprofessional) with little reference to fundamentals in the short to medium term. Ironically, when the market is in agreement about prices (extreme uniformity), it most often gets it wrong, exactly when believers in EMH say the investor should be getting it right. After all, if the majority of investors is wrong at these turning points, then they are chronic *mispricers* of markets, hardly what the efficient markets theory would have us believe.

APPENDIX A

MetaStock Formula Language Code

SQUEEZE PLAY I

```
Enter long:
(HHV(Fml("EMA5-21"),1) < 0)
AND (HHV(Fml("EMA5-21"),2) > 0)
AND C > Ref(H,-1)
Close long:
HHV(Fml("EMA21-50"),1)<0 and
HHV(Fml("EMA21-50"),2)>0
Enter short:
(LLV(Fml("EMA5-21"),1) > 0) and
AND (LLV(Fml("EMA5-21"),2) < 0)
AND C < Ref(L,-1)
Close short:
LLV(Fml("EMA21-50"),1)<0 and
LLV(Fml("EMA21-50"),2) < 0)
AND (HHV(Fml("EMA5-21"),2) > 0)
Positions: Long, Short
Entry trade price: Open
Entry trade delay: 1 (enters on next open)
Exit trade price: Open
Exit trade delay: 1 (exits on next open)
```

Note: System reverses with long and short signals.

SQUEEZE PLAY II

```
Enter long:
(HHV(Fml("EMA50-100"),10) > 5
```

```
AND Ref(C,1) > HHV(H,3)
Close long: (LLV(Fml("EMA50-100"),10) < -5)
Enter short:
(LLV(Fml("EMA50-100"),10) < -5)
AND Ref(C,1) < LLV(L,3)
Close short: (HHV(Fml("EMA50-100"),10) > 5)
Positions: Long, Short
Entry trade price: Open
Entry trade delay:2
Exit trade price: Open
Exit trade delay: 1
```

Note: Some versions of Squeeze Play II use alternative price triggers that are not included with this code. Appendix B does not contain Easy-Language® code for Squezze Play II.

TSUNAMI SENTIMENT WAVE

```
Enter long: (HHV(Fml("EMA21-50"),1) > 10)
Exit long: C
Enter short: (LLV(Fml("EMA21-50"),1) < -10)
Exit short: C
Positions: Long, Short
Entry trade price: Open
Entry trade delay: 1 (enters on next open)
Exit trade price: Open
Exit trade delay: 30, 60, 90 days
```

NEWS FLOW TESTING CODE

```
Enter long:
(HHV(Fml("EMA4-8"),2) > 5)
AND C > Ref(H,-1)
Close long: C
Enter short:
(LLV(Fml("EMA4-8"),2) < -5)
AND C < Ref(L,-1)
Close short: C
Positions: Long, short
Entry trade price: Open
```

```
Entry trade delay: 1 (enters on next open)
Exit trade price: Open
Exit trade delay: 1,2,3,4
```

Note: EMA4-8 processes a raw bear news intensity index, a normalized value using bear news and total Wall Street news.

ADVISORY OPINION TEST CODE

AAII and *Investors Intelligence* % Bears (Weekly)

```
Enter long:
(HHV(Fml("EMA1-4"),1) > 5)
AND C > Ref(H,-1)
Close long:
(LLV(Fml("EMA1-4"),1) < 0)
AND C < Ref(L,-1)
Enter short:
(LLV(Fml("EMA1-4"),1) < -5)
AND C < Ref(L,-1)
Close short:
(HHV(Fml("EMA1-4"),1) > 0)
AND C > Ref(H,-1)
Positions: Long and short
Entry trade price: Open
Entry trade delay: 1 (enters on next open)
Exit trade price: Open
Exit trade delay: 1 (exits on next open)
```

Market Vane's *Bullish Consensus* Weekly Index (S&P 500)

```
Enter long:
(LLV(Fml("EMA1-4"),1) < -5)
AND C > Ref(H,-1)
Close long:
(HHV(Fml("EMA1-4"),1) > 5)
AND C < Ref(L,-1)
Enter short:
(HHV(Fml("EMA1-4"),1) > 5)
AND C < Ref(L,-1)
Close short:
```

```
(LLV(Fml("EMA1-4"),1) < -5)
AND C > Ref(H,-1)
Positions: Long and short
Entry trade price: Open
Entry trade delay: 1 (enters on next open)
Exit trade price: Open
Exit trade delay: 1 (exits on next open)
```

CUSTOMER INDICATORS

EMA5-21 Custom Indicator Code

```
(((Ref((Mov(Security("symbol",C),5,E)),-1)-
Ref((Mov(Security("symbol",C),21,E)),-1))/
(Ref((Mov(Security("symbol",C),21,E)),-1)))*100)
```

EMA10-21 Custom Indicator Code

```
(((Ref((Mov(Security("symbol",C),10,E)),-1)-
Ref((Mov(Security("symbol",C),21,E)),-1))/
(Ref((Mov(Security("symbol",C),21,E)),-1)))*100)
```

EMA21-50 Custom Indicator Code

```
(((Ref((Mov(Security("symbol",C),21,E)),-1)-
Ref((Mov(Security("symbol",C),50,E)),-1))/
(Ref((Mov(Security("symbol",C),50,E)),-1)))*100)
```

EMA50-100 Custom Indicator Code

```
(((Ref((Mov(Security("symbol",C),50,E)),-1)-
Ref((Mov(Security("symbol",C),100,E)),-1))/
(Ref((Mov(Security("symbol",C),100,E)),-1)))*100)
End
```

APPENDIX B

TradeStation EasyLanguage® Code*

SENTIMENT OSCILLATOR FUNCTION

Inputs: The inputs are simply the length of the faster moving average and the length of the slower moving average.

Inputs for the fast and slow values are 5/21, 10/21, 21/50, 50/100.

This function can be used for an indicator, and is used in the trading systems presented in the book.

```
Inputs: FastAvgLength(numeric),
SlowAvgLength(numeric), Price(numeric);

Variables: nSlowXMA(0), nFastXMA(0);

nFastXMA = XAverage(Price, FastAvgLength);
nSlowXMA = XAverage(Price, SlowAvgLength);

SentimentOsc = ((nFastXMA - nSlowXMA)/(nSlowXMA)) *
100;
```

*All code was adapted for TradeStation by Ron Hudson (www.symmetrading.com). For questions or comments about TradeStation EasyLanguage® code for these systems, send an email to: jsumma264@cs.com. Ron Hudson or John Summa assume no responsibility for coding errors. Please verify all code by visiting TradingAgainstTheCrowd.com.

SENTIMENT OSCILLATOR INDICATOR

Inputs: The inputs are simply the length of a faster moving average and the length of a slower moving average.

Inputs for the fast and slow values are 5/21, 10/21, 21/50, 50/100. It is used with a daily sentiment data series, which is normally set up as Data2

```
Inputs: FastAvgLength(5), SlowAvgLength(21);

Plot1(SentimentOsc(FastAvgLength, SlowAvgLength,
Close), ("SentimentOsc");
```

SQUEEZE PLAY I SYSTEM (TRADESTATION EASYLANGUAGE® CODE

```
// Inputs are two exponential moving average lengths
Inputs: FastAvgLength(5), SlowAvgLength(21);

// Simplify code by using variables to signal bullish/bearish conditions
Variables: bBullishSignal(False), bBullExit2(False)
bBearExit2(False);
bBearishSignal(False);

// Skip first bar on chart to avoid divide by zero error
If BarNumber > 1 Then Begin

// Reset the flag variables and re-evaluate the signal each day
bBullishSignal = False;
bBearishSignal = False;
bBullExit2 = False;
bBearExit2 = False;

// Bullish if yesterday's SentimentOsc is negative, but the previous day's
SentimentOsc was positive
// Bearish if yesterday's SentimentOsc is positive, but the previous day's
SentimentOsc was negative
bBullishSignal = (SentimentOsc(FastAvgLength,
SlowAvgLength, Close of Data2)[1] < 0
```

```
And SentimentOsc(FastAvgLength, SlowAvgLength, Close
of Data2)[2] > 0);
bBearishSignal = (SentimentOsc(FastAvgLength,
SlowAvgLength, Close of Data2)[1] > 0
And SentimentOsc(FastAvgLength, SlowAvgLength, Close
of Data2)[2] < 0);

// Enter long if bullish signal and today closes higher than yesterday's high
If bBullishSignal And Close > High[1] Then Buy Next
Bar On Open;
// Enter short if bearish signal and today closes lower than yesterday's low
If bBearishSignal And Close < Low[1] Then Sell Short
Next Bar on Open;

// Additional Exit based on 21-50 oscillator
bBullExit2 = (SentimentOsc(21,50,High of Data2[1] < 0
And SentimentOsc(21,50,High of Data2)[2] > 0;
bBearExit2 = (SentimentOsc(21,50,Low of Data2[1] > 0
And SentimentOsc(21,50,Low of Data2)[2] < 0;

// Exit if long and bearish signal, or if short and bullish signal
If MarketPosition = 1 And (bBearishSignal or
bBullExit2) Then Sell Next Bar On Open;
If MarketPosition = -1 And (bBullishSignal or
bBearExit2)Then BuyToCover Next Bar On Open;

End;
```

ORIGINAL METASTOCK CODE

Squeeze Play I

```
Enter long:
(HHV(Fml("EMA5-21"),1) < 0)
AND (HHV(Fml("EMA5-21"),2) > 0)
AND C > Ref(H,-1)
Close long:
(HHV(Fml("EMA21-50"),1) > 0)
AND (HHV(Fml("EMA21-50"),2) < 0)
Enter short:
```

```
(HHV(Fml("EMA5-21"),1) > 0)
AND (HHV(Fml("EMA5-21"),2) < 0)
AND C > Ref(H,-1)
Close short:
(HHV(Fml("EMA21-50"),1) < 0)
AND (HHV(Fml("EMA21-50"),2) > 0)

Positions: Long, Short
Entry trade price: Open
Entry trade delay: 1
Exit trade price: Open
Exit trade delay: 1
```

TSUNAMI SENTIMENT WAVE SYSTEM (TRADESTATION EASYLANGUAGE® CODE

Note that this System requires two data streams.

```
// Inputs are two exponential moving average lengths.
Inputs: FastAvgLength(21), SlowAvgLength(50);

// Simplify code by using variables to signal bullish/bearish conditions
Variables: bBullishSignal(False),
bBearishSignal(False);

// Skip first bar on chart to avoid divide by zero error
If BarNumber > 1 Then Begin

// Reset the flag variables and re-evaluate the signal each day
bBullishSignal = False;
bBearishSignal = False;

// Bullish if yesterday's SentimentOsc is greater than 10
// Bearish if yesterday's SentimentOsc is less than –10
bBullishSignal = (Highest SentimentOsc(FastAvgLength,
SlowAvgLength, Close of Data,2),1 > 10);
bBearishSignal = (Lowest SentimentOsc(FastAvgLength,
SlowAvgLength, Close of Data,2),1 < -10);

// Enter long on tomorrow's open if bullish signal
If bBullishSignal Then Buy Next Bar On Open;
```

// Enter short on tomorrow's open if bearish signal
```
If bBearishSignal Then Sell Short Next Bar on Open;
```

// Exit on the close for a one-day trade
```
If MarketPosition = 1 Then Sell This Bar On Close;
If MarketPosition = -1 Then BuyToCover This Bar On
Close;

End;
```

ORIGINAL METASTOCK CODE

Tsunami Sentiment Wave

```
Enter long: (HHV(Fml("EMA21-50"),1) > 10)
Exit long: C
Enter short: (LLV(Fml("EMA21-50"),1) < -10)
Exit short: C

Positions: Long, Short
Entry trade price: Open
Entry trade delay: 1
Exit trade price: Open
Exit trade delay: 30, 60, 90 days
```

NEWSFLOW TESTING CODE (TRADESTATION EASYLANGUAGE® CODE

Note that this System requires two data streams.

// Inputs are two exponential moving average lengths.
```
Inputs: FastAvgLength(4), SlowAvgLength(8);
```

// Simplify code by using variables to signal bullish/bearish setups
Variables: bBullishSignal(False),
```
bBearishSignal(False);
```

// Skip first bar on chart to avoid divide by zero error
```
If BarNumber > 1 Then Begin
```

```
// Reset the flag variables and re-evaluate the signal each day
bBullishSignal = False;
bBearishSignal = False;

// Bullish if the highest value for the SentimentOsc over the last 2 days is greater than 5
// Bearish if the lowest value for the SentimentOsc over the last 2 days is less than –5
bBullishSignal = (Highest(SentimentOsc(FastAvgLength,
SlowAvgLength, Close of Data2), 2) > 5);
bBearishSignal = (Lowest(SentimentOsc(FastAvgLength,
SlowAvgLength, Close of Data2), 2) < -5);

// Enter long on tomorrow's open if bullish signal
If bBullishSignal Then Buy Next Bar On Open;
// Enter short on tomorrow's open if bearish signal
If bBearishSignal Then Sell Short Next Bar on Open;

// Exit on the close*
If MarketPosition = 1 Then Sell This Bar On Close;
If MarketPosition = -1 Then BuyToCover This Bar On
Close;

End;
```

*This will need to be programmed to delay exit by T + 30, T + 60, and T + 90 day.

ORIGINAL METASTOCK CODE NEWSFLOW TESTING CODE*

```
Enter long:
(HHV(Fml("EMA4-8"),2) > 5)
AND  C > Ref(H,-1)
Close long: C
Enter short:
(LLV(Fml("EMA4-8"),2) < -5)
AND C < Ref(L,-1)
Close short: C
Positions: Long, short
Entry trade price: Open
Entry trade delay: 1
Exit trade price: Open
Exit trade delay: 1,2,3,4 weeks
```

*Uses weekly data

ADVISORY OPINION TESTING CODE (TRADESTATION EASYLANGUAGE® CODE)

AAII and Investors Intelligence % Bears

Note that this System requires two data streams.

```
// Inputs are two exponential moving average lengths.
Inputs: FastAvgLength(1), SlowAvgLength(4);

// Simplify code by using variables to signal bullish/bearish conditions
Variables: bBullishSignal(False),
bBearishSignal(False);
// Skip first bar on chart to avoid divide by zero error
If BarNumber > 1 Then Begin

// Reset the flag variables and re-evaluate the signal each day
bBullishSignal = False;
bBearishSignal = False;

// Bullish if SentimentOsc is greater than 5 on close previous day
// Bearish if SentimentOsc is less than –5 on close previous day
bBullishSignal = (SentimentOsc(FastAvgLength,
SlowAvgLength, Close of Data2)[1] > 5);
bBearishSignal = (SentimentOsc(FastAvgLength,
SlowAvgLength, Close of Data2)[1] < -5);

// Enter long on tomorrow's open if bullish signal and close is greater than
yesterday's high
If bBullishSignal And Close > High[1] Then Buy Next
Bar On Open;
// Enter short on tomorrow's open if bearish signal and close is lower than
yesterday's low
If bBearishSignal And Close < Low[1] Then Sell Short
Next Bar on Open;

// Exit long on the close if SentimentOsc is below zero on previous day
close and today's close is lower than yesterday's low
If MarketPosition = 1 And SentimentOsc(FastAvgLength,
SlowAvgLength, Close of Data2)[1] < 0
And Close < Low[1] Then Sell This Bar On Close;
// Exit short on the close if SentimentOsc is above zero on previous day
close and today's close is higher than yesterday's high
```

```
If MarketPosition = -1 And SentimentOsc(FastAvgLength,
SlowAvgLength, Close of Data2)[1] > 0
And Close > High[1] Then BuyToCover This Bar On Close;

End;
```

*Uses weekly data

ORIGINAL METASTOCK CODE

AAII and Investors Intelligence % Bears*

```
Enter long:
(HHV(Fml("EMA1-4"),1) > 5)
AND C > Ref(H,-1)
Close long:
(LLV(Fml("EMA1-4"),1) < 0)
AND C < Ref(L,-1)
Enter short:
(LLV(Fml("EMA1-4"),1) < -5)
AND C < Ref(L,-1)
Close short:
(HHV(Fml("EMA1-4"),1) > 0)
AND C > Ref(H,-1)

Positions: Long and short
Entry trade price: Open
Entry trade delay: 1
Exit trade price: Open
Exit trade delay: 1
```

*Uses weekly data

ADVISORY OPINION TESTING CODE II (TRADESTATION EASYLANGUAGE® CODE)

Market Vane's Bullish Consensus Weekly Index (S&P 500)

Note that this System requires two data streams.

```
// Inputs are two exponential moving average lengths.
Inputs: FastAvgLength(1), SlowAvgLength(4);
```

```
// Simplify code by using variables to signal bullish/bearish conditions
Variables: bBullishSignal(False),
bBearishSignal(False);

// Skip first bar on chart to avoid divide by zero error
If BarNumber > 1 Then Begin

// Reset the flag variables and re-evaluate the signal each day
bBullishSignal = False;
bBearishSignal = False;
// Bullish if the highest value for the SentimentOsc over the last 2 days is
greater than 5
// Bearish if the lowest value for the SentimentOsc over the last 2 days
is less than –5
bBullishSignal = (Lowest(SentimentOsc(FastAvgLength,
SlowAvgLength, Close of Data2), 1) < -5);
bBearishSignal = (Highest(SentimentOsc(FastAvgLength,
SlowAvgLength, Close of Data2), 1) > 5);

// Enter long on tomorrow's open if bullish signal
If bBullishSignal And Close > High[1] Then Buy Next
Bar On Open;
// Enter short on tomorrow's open if bearish signal
If bBearishSignal And Close < Low[1] Then Sell Short
Next Bar on Open;

// Exit on the close
If MarketPosition = 1 And bBearishSignal
And Close < Low[1] Then Sell This Bar On Close;
If MarketPosition = -1 And bBullishSignal
And Close > High[1] Then BuyToCover This Bar On Close;

End;
```

ORIGINAL METASTOCK CODE

Market Vane's Bullish Consensus Weekly Index (S&P 500)

```
Enter long:
(LLV(Fml("EMA1-4"),1) < -5)
AND C > Ref(H,-1)
Close long:
```

```
(HHV(Fml("EMA1-4"),1) > 5)
AND  C < Ref(L,-1)
Enter short:
(HHV(Fml("EMA1-4"),1) > 5)
AND C < Ref(L,-1)
Close short:
(LLV(Fml("EMA1-4"),1) < -5)
AND C > Ref(H,-1)
Positions: Long and short
Entry trade price: Open
Entry trade delay: 1
Exit trade price: Open
Exit trade delay: 1
```

Note: All of the above strategies must be applied to a TradeStation chart with two data streams, the second of which should be a symbol like $WPCVE (CBOE equity put/call ratio), for example.

APPENDIX C

Notes on System Testing

After completing a draft of this book, I thought readers would benefit from a primer on interpreting Equis MetaStock Professional (version 7.2) system tests, given that so many tests are presented and discussed that use the software. Therefore, I have included a brief explanation of the test variables as well as some comments on testing methodology. Because I do not use TradeStation, I do not include comments on that program. Appendix B, however, has TradeStation code for some of the systems presented in this book.

The most important category, although hardly sufficient on its own for performance analysis, is *total net profit*. This value, which is a dollar figure for tests done on stocks and a total point gain for futures, includes the system performance resulting from all previously *closed* trades as well as any gain or loss on *open* positions for the entire period of the data sample. While the time frames are as long as nine years in some of the tests in this book, they do not include a measure of interest opportunity costs (interest earnings foregone) in the total net profit for stock system trades, nor the interest that is earned on margin money held in Treasury bills for trading systems using futures.

Once total net profit is known, the MetaStock calculates the *percentage gain/loss*. This percentage number, however, is not calculated for trading system tests on futures markets, which is why I calculate it manually for the reader in many of the chapters. The percentage gain/loss is calculated on an annual and total basis. This value for system tests on stocks or stock indices is calculated by the MetaStock Professional based on two variables: *total net profit* and *initial investment*. This is done by taking the total net profit as a percentage of the initial investment. Initial investment, however, is only applicable to stocks. Futures require an assumption about initial account value, usually based on minimum requirements or some minimum account size to specify an initial investment for manually deriving a percentage return.

For stocks, it is the amount of cash invested at the start of the test, and this can be indicated at the outset of testing. In this book, all tests done on stocks have a specified beginning balance of $10,000, and most are traded with a 50 percent margin account. Because futures are inherently a leveraged derivative (with each market having different leverage ratios based on contract values and margin requirements), futures simply get tested, as mentioned above, based on a point gain/loss basis. This is an important difference for the stock testing and tests done on futures, and it has implications for the money management dimension.

If a stock position is entered and closed with a gain, the gain is reflected in the total equity (and equity plot, see below). For example, a beginning account investment of $10,000 might show $10,500 after a winning trade. When the next trade is entered, however, the entire amount is invested and the rate of profit gain or loss is calculated on $10,500, not the initial $10,000. This allows for compounding returns at sometimes phenomenal rates, but also can lead to equally drastic drops in equity. By no means is this the only way to undertake money management; an entire book could be devoted to this subject. I simply assume for the sake of simplicity that all available capital is always invested for stocks; the system tests allow only one fixed setting. In other words, it is not possible to increase or decrease position sizes given different outcomes of the system equity plot.

That said, when using the points-only tests on futures, there is no such compounding. Each trade assumes a one-lot size, which means the gains (if there are any) do not get compounded in the form of larger positions (or smaller ones, if declining equity follows a series of losing trades) when a new trade signal is generated. If the system is doing very well, it is understating its potential equity if no compounding of gains is built into the trading program. Clearly, given some of the very high triple-digit returns from some of the system tests using no compounding, and given the stable equity plots, even a small degree of compounding of gains would lead to dramatic improvements in equity growth. Again, MetaStock Professional limits this ability, although it is certainly possible to produce a simulated compounded equity plot with the data using Microsoft Excel, something I do not undertake here.

Finally, commissions are only deducted for system tests on stocks that have a large number of trades, as this can become a significant portion of transaction costs.

BUY/HOLD PROFIT

When a system generates a positive *total net profit* and positive *percent gain*, it may still not be sufficient for actual trading. The most important necessary condition for a good trading system is that the *total net profit* be better than the *buy/hold profit* and profit rate. Buy-and-hold profit is simple to understand. It is the profit or loss from entering a hypothetical position at the beginning of the sample period of a back test and held until the end of that period. The results of such a position are then compared with the system test results.

A system test should be able to beat the *buy/hold profit* to be a worthwhile system. This may not always be the case, as it does not actually look at a reward/risk dimension. The equity plot, for example, may be smooth and steadily trending upward, but still may not beat the buy/hold approach. However, the buy/hold equity might be extremely volatile, dropping sometimes by large amounts before finishing higher, which must be taken into account. To get a true picture of the buy/hold approach in relationship to the system *total net profit*, therefore, it is important to account for volatility of earnings, which is not an area I explore here. For short trades only, it is important to compare results with negative *buy/hold profit*, since a positive short/hold profit would be captured in a negative value for the *buy/hold profit* performance. And a negative short/hold profit would be captured with a positive *buy/hold profit*. Finally, a *buy/hold percentage gain/loss* for the initial investment (stocks only) is calculated for direct comparison with a trading system annual and total *percentage gain/loss*.

When *total net profit* is calculated, it is possible to determine *average profit per trade*, which is computed by dividing *total net profit* by total *closed* and *open* trades. A related criterion is *average win/average loss ratio*. The *average win* measure is based on all *winning* (closed) trade profits and divides this value by the total number of *winning* (closed) trades. *Average loss*, meanwhile, is computed similarly, using total losses in the numerator and total losing trades in the denominator; open trade balances, however, are not counted. Since there can be substantial gains or losses on open positions, it is important to evaluate these to see if they are large enough to distort the variables. Therefore, the *amount of winning trades* minus the *amount of losing trades* may not equal the *total net profit*.

DRAWDOWN AND LOSS ANALYSIS

I consider the number of consecutive losing trades an important variable. While *total losing trades* and *amount of losing trades* are important, any system that has more than three consecutive losing trades is not one that I would like to use. Additionally, it is always important to look at the *largest loss* variable, which measures the least profitable closed trade. Even though *total net profit* beats *buy/hold profit*, a large loss can be devastating to equity, depending on when that loss occurs.

Maximum system close drawdown and *maximum system open drawdown* are probably the most important variables to monitor in system testing. The former represents the largest drop in equity relative to the initial investment that occurs from positions already closed. This tells us how much the system lost from the point of view of total starting equity once at the point of closing any trade. Many of the systems tested in this book have zero closed system drawdowns, which mean equity never reached a negative level. However, a large *maximum open trade drawdown* can wipe out a lot of equity even if it is not below initial equity.

Maximum system open drawdown simply looks at equity drops taking into account any open trades. An open and closed trade may have a large drawdown and then end up a winner. *Maximum system open drawdown* is therefore more important in my view than *maximum closed system drawdown* because it provides us with more information about the system behavior. This is especially important for futures traders, who are margined day to day by settlement prices of futures contracts. An open position drawdown might trigger massive margin calls to stay in the position. A look at just the *maximum system closed drawdown* would not let us know this. These maximum drawdown variables in conjunction with the largest loss variable provide a likely worst-case view of the system performance, which helps in developing the correct money management required to trade the system.

PROFIT/LOSS ASSESSMENT

Finally, we want to know how much winning trades make in comparison to losing trades, which is captured by the *profit/loss index*. This index combines winning and losing trades into a single number that ranges from –100 (system worst) to +100 (system best).

When the index is negative, the system produces a net profit loss. A positive index indicates a positive net profit. Consequently, a perfect score would be generated when there are no losses and all wins. And all losses and no winning trades would produce an index of –100.

Another assessment of profit occurs with the *reward/risk index*. Looking at reward relative to risk, this index is calculated using the lowest point of the equity line below the initial investment and the final point on the equity line. Like the previous index, this one ranges between –100 and +100. Smooth equity plots get a very high index number, which we saw in many of the trading systems presented in this book.

Finally, the *buy/hold index* shows the trading system's profits as a percentage of the *buy/hold profits*. Most of the systems tested in this book managed to score an index value greater than 100, meaning the buy/hold profit was exceeded by the trading system *total net profits*. This is the ultimate objective of trading systems.

Index

T